COMPUTER HARDWARE ESSENTIALS

PRACTICAL GUIDE

Analyst Odion J. O. Okundia

Computer Hardware Essentials Practical Guide

© **Analyst. Odion J. O. Okundia**

2nd Edition, March 17th, 2017

DEDICATION

I dedicate this book to Chief (Dr.) Christopher Pere Katimi Iredia Ekiyor, the Oracle of Niger Deltans. A Youth leader par Excellence and also the brain behind amnesty programme in Nigeria, CEO and founder, RAHI MEDICAL OUTREACH.

ACKNOWLEDGEMENTS

My first and foremost gratitude goes to the CEO and Founder, Microsoft Corporation, Bill Gate and the Senior Special Adviser on Legislative Matter to the Speaker, EDHA, Hon. Tony Osazuwa. Since the scholars and authors are too many to be mentioned individually here, I hope that the references that I made to them and their works in different sections of this book convey my sincere recognition and appreciation of their significant positive influence in my writing this book.

I wish to express special gratitude to my parents, Mr and Mrs Godwin Omoruyi Okundia; Rev. Oje Ohiwerei; Mr. Jonathan Osunde; Engr. Alfred Erick-Etchie; Mr. Eghosa A. Okundia; Hon. Austin Gengenu; Mr. Moses Igwu; Mr. Patrick Ege; Mr. Iboi Festus; Mr. Tony Dudu; Mr. Abel Ogboi; Dr. Emmanuel Egharevba; Mr. Osarenkhoe B. Efe; Mr. Terence Omon Osifoh; Patricia Izevbizua; Phillip Oke Topa and Emmanuel Oronsaye.

Indeed, I appreciate the support and encouragement I received from the following people: Mr. Osaretin Osarenkhoe; Mr. Efe Amuboh; Nat Osifoh; Mr. Watson Iluedo; Engr. Theophilus Okeremute Iguyovwe; Miss Yvonne Ivie Okundia; Mr. & Mrs Festus Akhator; Mr. Efe Igbuzor; Mr. Jude Amadin; Peter Odion John; Paul Akhere John; Emmanuel and Philip Illah; Mr. Austin Agbonlahor; Heritage Theatre Ministry, Edo Youth Political Vanguard; and Twins Association of Nigeria (TAN). They have been sources of inspiration to me during this project. They provided me with decisive and moral support towards the end of this work which enabled me to actually complete it.

I am profoundly grateful to Mr. Solomon Chuks Ejiro Nsumei, my Project Manager and for reawakening my spirit to complete this book and to all my students, trainees and fans, I say thanks a million for the contributions, love and guidance throughout the period of the preparation of this book.

Analyst Odion J. O. Okundia

PREFACE

It has been noted that Information Technology is the live-wire of the global village we are living in today. This makes it important that every individual must be well equipped with the basic knowledge of Computer and Information Technology in order to join the moving train of Information Technology. This need cannot be over-emphasized because there is no field in human endeavour today that computer is not applied. Even job seekers these days are required to have the basic knowledge of computer science and information technology.

This book is designed to bring closer computer and information technology to the teeming population of those who wish to be computer literate. It is arranged in an understandable manner with illustrative pictures and diagrams.

It has six chapters. Chapters one to two focused on: Identification of Computer and Computer Assembling. Chapters three and four treat: Microsoft Windows; Preventive Maintenance and Troubleshooting.

While in the concluding chapters five and six, the readers will be introduced to Principles of Networking and Network Security.

The contents of this book make it useful for those in Information Technology and Non-Information Technology disciplines who seek for knowledge of Computer and Information Technology and the desire to improve on it.

Analyst Odion J. O. Okundia

FOREWORD

The task of writing a standard and acceptable textbook is not an easy one as it requires proper reasoning, concentration, in-dept research work, gathering of resource information as well as presentation of such ideas and sourced materials in a logical sequence. Put together, I congratulate this promising author for putting together this scholarly text.

After editing this work, I am very delighted to write a foreword on this text well titled **"Computer Hardware Essentials and Practical Guide"** written by Computer **Analyst Odion J. O. Okundia.**

The author has exhibited a lot of intelligence, maturity, competence and well researched work on this course under review. Evidence of this is his skillful discussions on the following topics: Identification of Computer Components; Computer Assembling; Microsoft Windows; Preventive Maintenance and Troubleshooting; Principles of Networking and Network Security.

The book is self explanatory, educative and informative with pictures of the computer hardware, software and related issues discussed in this book which will facilitate teaching, learning and understanding of the topics treated.
At the end of each chapter, there are revision questions to guide and test the students understanding of the topics treated.

Also covered in this text are the syllabi of National Board for Technical Education (NBTE), National Commission for Colleges of Education (NCCE) on this course under reference. Again, Diploma and undergraduate students of the Nigerian universities will find this book very helpful in their academic programmes.

Honestly, the effort of the author is worthy of commendation as his contributions on this field of study will enhance knowledge and proper understanding of Computer Science and Information Technology.

In view of the above, the book is highly recommended to students and lecturers in the institutions of higher learning.

Nicholas Ogini, *M.NCS, MCPN*
(B.Sc., M.Sc. and Ph.D Computer Science)
Head of Computer Science Unit
Department of Maths/Computer Science,
Delta State University, Abraka, Nigeria.

COMPLEMENTARY FOREWORD

Many technical books written these days are often so difficult to understand because the authors tend to forget that these books exist to serve students who might not yet be fully conversant with the topics at hand. In COMPUTER HARDWARE ESSENTIALS Practical guide, System and Technical Analyst Odion J. O. Okundia has taken great pains to carefully guide a student, from the very basics, right up to more advanced concepts.

Using detailed explanations and illustrations to teach and educate, Odion J. O. Okundia has demonstrated clear mastery of the subject at hand. I particularly love the gradually increasing amount of information the Author gently brings to the subject matter and see it as a clear victory for those students who are fortunate enough to lay their hands on a copy of this book and read it. Buy it, but more importantly study it from cover to cover, you will be greatly rewarded for your effort.

ENGR. THEOPHILUS OKEREMUTE IGUYOVWE
MANAGER ING BANK
NETHERLANDS

This book is an excellent source of the practical and fundamental knowledge needed in understanding basic computer Architecture as well as an indepth introductory description of the integrated Circuits needed for computer networking.
Additionally, I believe lecturers and Institutions looking to provide practical guidance and examples for the next generation of Software Engineers and Technical IT Professionals, would be delighted to own a copy of this book, as they would find it greatly reduces the burden of not only creating learning material, but provides a wide reservoir of examples, tips and methods.

CHARLES OSARO ONAGHISE
PRODUCTION ENGINEER
INTEL CORP,
SANTA CLARA, CALIFORNIA, USA.

Computer Hardware Essentials Practical Guide written by Odion J.O Okundia contains very concise practical approach to computer hardware for students and those interested in being part of the IT industry. It also contains pictures and questions that will lock or easily disseminate all its information in of what it talks about. The approach of the book and language is easy to understand.

Getting the book, I believe would put one step ahead with its containing audio cd/mp3/mp4 to guide for any eventuality and can serve as self-help to the user. I believe this resource is balanced enough to help anyone interested in computer hardware.

EHIGOBOCHIE AMENAWON,
B.Sc, MCITP, MCSE, MCT, MTA, MCP, MCSA.
Faculty/Engineer
NIIT BENIN,
11 Adesuwa Road, GRA, Benin City.

TABLE OF CONTENTS

CHAPTER ONE

IDENTIFICATION OF COMPUTER COMPONENTS

1.1 COMPUTER SYSTEM

A computer system consist of hardware and software components. **Computer Hardware** is the physical components or equipment which can be seen, touched and felt. They consist of casing, cables, speakers, storage drives, keyboards, monitors, printers, etc. The term **computer software** includes the operating system and programs. The operating system instructs the computer on how to operate. These operations may include identifying, accessing, and processing information. Programs or applications perform different functions. Programs vary widely, depending on the type of information that is being accessed or generated. For example, instructions for balancing a check book is very different from instructions for simulating a virtual-reality world on the Internet.

The following sections discussed the hardware components found in a computer system.

1.2 CASING AND POWER SUPPLIES

The computer case provides protection and support for the computer's internal components. All computers need a power supply to convert alternating-current (AC) power from the wall socket into direct-current (DC) power. The size and shape of the computer casing is usually determined by the motherboard and other internal components. You can select a large computer casing to accommodate additional components that may be required in the future. Other users may select a smaller one that requires minimal space. In general, the computer case should be durable and easy to service and should have enough room for expansion.

The power supply must provide enough power for the components that are currently installed and allow for additional components that may be added later. If you choose a power supply that powers only the current components, it may be necessary to replace the power supply when other components are upgraded.

After completing this section, you will meet these objectives:

♦ Casing.
♦ Power Supplies.

Casing

A computer casing also contains the framework to support a computer's internal components while providing an enclosure for added protection. Computer cases typically are made of plastic, steel, and aluminium that are available in a variety of styles. The size and layout of a case is called a *form factor*. There are many types of cases, but the basic form factors for computer cases include desktop and tower. Desktop cases may be slim line or full-sized, and tower cases may be mini or full. The back of the case holds the vast majority of the system unit connections. You will also notice the power supply almost always at the top of the case distinguished by its cooling fan and power plug. Note that one area of the back, the I/O area, holds all of the on board connections, while another area in the back contains slots for cards. Similarly, the case uses slots to enable access to the external connectors on cards installed in the system unit.

Figure 1.1 Tower Cases

Computer cases are referred to in a number of ways:

♦   Housing
♦   Tower
♦   Box
♦   Cabinet
♦   Computer chassis

In addition to providing protection and support, cases also provide an environment designed to keep the internal components cool. Case fans are used to move air through the computer case. As the air passes into the components, it absorbs heat and then exits the case. This process keeps the computer's components from overheating. You must consider many factors when choosing a case:

♦   The size of the motherboard

♦   The number of external or internal drive locations, called bays

♦   Available space when choosing a computer case, consider the following:

♦   **Model Type:** There are two main case models. One type is for desktop PCs, and the other is for tower computers. The type of motherboard you choose determines the type of case that can be used. The size and shape must match exactly.

♦   **Size:** If a computer has many components, it needs more room for airflow to keep the system cool.

♦   **Available Space:** Desktop cases allow space conservation in tight areas, because the monitor can be placed on top of the unit. The design of the desktop case may limit the number and size of the components that can be added.

♦   **Power Supply:** You must match the power rating and connection type of the power supply to the type of motherboard you have chosen.

♦   **Appearance:** Some people don't care for how the case looks. You have many case designs to choose from if you want an attractive case.

♦   **Status Display:** What is going on inside the case can be very important. LED indicators that are mounted in the front of the case can tell you if the system is receiving power, when the hard drive is being used, and when the computer is on standby or sleeping.

♦   **Vents:** All cases have a vent on the power supply, and some have another vent on the back to help draw air into or out of the system. Some cases are designed with more vents in the event that the system needs a way to dissipate an unusual amount of heat. This situation may occur when many devices are installed close together in the case. In addition to providing protection from the environment, cases help prevent damage from static electricity.   Internal components of the computer are grounded by attachment to the case.

Note

You should select a case that matches the physical dimensions of the power supply and motherboard.

♦   **Power Supplies**

The power supply, shown in Figure 1-2, converts alternating-Current (AC) power coming from a wall outlet into direct-Current (DC) power, which is a lower voltage. DC power is required for all the components inside the computer.

Figure 1.2: Power Supply

Most connectors today are keyed connectors. Keyed connectors are designed to be inserted in only one direction. Each part of the connector has a coloured wire with a different voltage running through it, as described in different power supply, form factors provide different power output connections, depending on the system requirements.

As form factors have been slowly phased out by ATX. Form factor power supplies because of the different case sizes and advanced features. ATXv12 was created to add power support for the motherboard by adding another four-pin power connector.

Note

Different connectors are used to connect specific components and various locations on the motherboard:

•   A Molex connector is a keyed connector used to connect to an optical drive or hard drive.

•   A Berg connector is a keyed connector used to connect to a floppy drive. A Berg connector is smaller than a Molex connector.

- A 20-pin or 24-pin slotted connector is used to connect to the motherboard. The 24-pin slotted connector has two rows of 12 pins each, and the 20-pin slotted connector has two rows of 10 pins each.

- A four-pin-to-eight-pin auxiliary power connector has two rows of two to four pins and supplies power to all the areas of the motherboard. The four-pin-to-eight-pin auxiliary power connector is the same shape as the main power connector, but smaller.

- Older standard power supplies used two connectors called P8 and P9 to connect to the motherboard. P8 and P9 were unkeyed connectors. They could be installed backwards, potentially damaging the motherboard or power supply. The installation required that the connectors were lined up with the black wires together in the middle.

Note

If you have a difficult time inserting a connector, try a different way, or check to make sure that no bent pins or foreign objects are on the way. Remember, if it seems difficult to plug in any cable or other part, something is wrong. Cables, connectors, and components are designed to fit together snugly. Never force any connector or component. Connectors that are plugged in incorrectly will damage the plug and the connector. Take your time, and make sure that you are handling the hardware correctly.

1.3   ELECTRICITY AND OHM'S LAW

The four basic parameters of electricity are:
- Voltage (V)
- Current (C)
- Power (P)
- Resistance (R)

Voltage Current, Power and Resistance are electronics terms that a computer technician must know:

- **Voltage** is a measure of the force required to push electrons through a circuit. Voltage is measured in volts (V). A computer power supply usually produces several different voltages.

- **Current** is a measure of the number of electrons going through a circuit. Current is measured in amperes, or amps (A). Computer power supplies deliver different amperages for each output voltage.

- **Power** is a measure of the pressure required to push electrons through a circuit, called voltage, multiplied by the number of electrons going through that circuit, called current. The measurement is called watts (W). Computer power supplies are rated in watts.

- **Resistance** is the opposition to the flow of current in a circuit. Resistance is measured in ohms. Lower resistance allows more current, and therefore more power, to flow through a circuit. A good fuse has low resistance or a measurement of almost 0 ohms.

This system produces the same power, but with less current. Computers normally use power supplies ranging from 200 W to 500 W. However, some Computers may need 500-W to 800-W power supplies. When building a computer, select a power supply with sufficient wattage to power all the components. Obtain the wattage information for the components from the manufacturer's documentation. When deciding on a power supply, be sure to choose a power supply that has enough power for the current components.

Caution

Do not open a power supply, electronic capacitors located inside a power supply can hold a charge for extended periods of time.

1.4   COMPUTER INTERNAL COMPONENTS

This section discusses the names and characteristics of a computer's internal components, as shown in Figure 1.3.

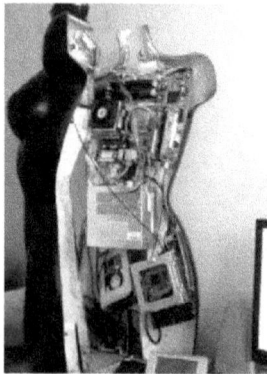

Fig. 1.3: Computer Internal Components

After completing this section, you will meet these objectives:

♦ Identification and knowing the characteristics of CPUs.

♦ Identification and characteristics of motherboards.

♦ Identification and characteristics of storage drives.

♦ Identification and characteristics of cooling systems.

♦ Identification and characteristics of adapter cards.

♦ Identification and characteristics of ROM and RAM.

♦ Identification and characteristics of internal cables.

CPUs

The ***Central Processing Unit (CPU)*** is considered the computer's brain. It is sometimes called the processor. Most processing and calculations take place in the CPU. In terms of computing power, the CPU is the most important element of a computer system. CPUs come in different form factors, each style requiring a particular slot or socket on the motherboard. Common CPU manufacturers include Intel and AMD. The CPU socket or slot is the connector that is the interface between the motherboard and the processor. Most CPU sockets and processors in use today are built around the Pin Grid Array (PGA) architecture, in which the pins on the underside of the processor are inserted into the socket, usually with Zero Insertion Force (ZIF). ZIF refers to the amount of force needed to install a CPU into the motherboard socket or slot. Slot-based processors are cartridge-shaped and fit into a slot that looks similar to an expansion slot.

The CPU executes a program, which is a sequence of stored instructions. Each model of processor has an instruction set, which it executes. The CPU executes the program by processing each piece of data as directed by the program and the instruction set. While the CPU is executing one step of the program, the remaining instructions and the data are stored nearby in a special memory called *cache*. Two major CPU architectures are related to instruction sets:

Reduced Instruction Set Computer (RISC): Architects use a relatively small set of instructions, and RISC chips are designed to execute these instructions very rapidly.

Complex Instruction Set Computer (CISC): Architectures use a broad set of instructions, resulting in fewer steps per operation. Some CPUs incorporate hyperthreading to enhance the CPU's performance. With *hyperthreading*, the CPU has multiple pieces of code being executed simultaneously on each pipeline. To an operating system, a single CPU with hyperthreading appears to be two CPUs. A CPU's power is measured by its speed and the amount of data it can process. A CPU's speed is rated in cycles per second. The speed of current CPUs is measured in millions of cycles per second, called megahertz (MHz), or billions of cycles per second, called gigahertz (GHz). The amount of data that a CPU can process at onetime depends on the size of the processor data bus. This is also called the CPU bus or the front-side bus (FSB).

The wider the processor data bus, the more powerful the processor. Current processors have a 32-bit or 64-bit processor data bus.

Overclocking is a technique used to make a processor work at a faster speed than its original specification. Overclocking is an unreliable way to improve computer performance and can damage the CPU.

MMX is a set of multimedia instructions built into Intel processors. MMX-enabled microprocessors can handle many common multimedia operations that normally are handled by a separate sound or video card. However, only software specially written to call MMX instructions can take advantage of the MMX instruction set.

The latest processor technology has caused CPU manufacturers to find ways to incorporate more than one CPU core into a single chip. Many CPUs can process multiple instructions concurrently:

Socket Pins Layout Voltage Supported Processors

Single-core CPU: One core inside a single CPU chip that handles all the processing capability. A motherboard manufacturer may provide sockets for more than a single processor, providing the ability to build a powerful multiprocessor computer.

Dual-core CPU: Two cores inside a single CPU chip, in which both cores can process information at the same time.

Motherboard

The motherboard is the main printed circuit board. It contains the buses, or electrical pathways, found in a computer. These buses allow data to travel between the various components that comprise a computer. A motherboard is also known as the system board, backplane, or main board. Figure 1-4 shows a variety of motherboards.

The motherboard accommodates the central processing unit (CPU), RAM, expansion slots, heat sink/fan assembly, BIOS chip, chip set, and the embedded wires that interconnect the motherboard components. Sockets, internal and external connectors, and various ports are also placed on the

Fig. 1.4: Mother Board

The form factor of motherboards pertains to the board's size and shape. It also describes the physical layout of the different components and devices on the motherboard. Motherboards have various form factors:

- Advanced Technology (AT)
- Advanced Technology Extended (ATX)
- Smaller footprint than Advanced Technology Extended (Mini-ATX)
- Smaller footprint than Advanced Technology Extended (Micro-ATX)
- Low-Profile Extended (LPX)
- New Low-Profile Extended (NLX)
- Balanced technology Extended (BTX)

An important set of components on the motherboard is the chip set. The chip set is composed of various integrated circuits attached to the motherboard that control how system hardware interacts with the CPU and motherboard. The CPU is installed into a slot or socket on the motherboard. The socket on the motherboard determines the type of CPU that can be installed.

The chip set of a motherboard allows the CPU to communicate and interact with the computer's other components and to exchange data with system memory (RAM), hard-disk drives, video cards, and other output devices. The chip set establishes how much memory can be added to a motherboard. The chip set also determines the type of connectors on the motherboard. Most chip sets are divided into two distinct components, northbridge and southbridge. What each component does varies from manufacturer to manufacturer, but in general the north bridge controls access to the RAM, video card, and the speeds at which the CPU can communicate with them. The video card is sometimes integrated into the northbridge. The southbridge, in most cases, allows the CPU to communicate with the hard drives, sound card, USB ports, and other input/output (I/O) ports.

Storage Drives

A storage drive reads or writes information to magnetic or optical storage media. It can be used to store data permanently or to retrieve information from a media disk. Storage drives can be installed inside the computer case, such as a hard drive. For portability, some storage drives can connect to the computer using a USB port, a FireWire port, or a SCSI port.

These portable storage drives are sometimes called removable drives and can be used on multiple computers. Figure 1.4 shows some common types of storage drives:

- Floppy drive
- Optical drive
- Flash drive
- Hard drive
- Network drive

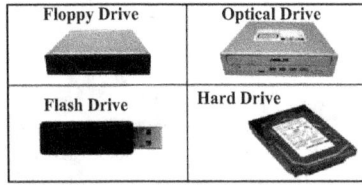

Fig. 1.5: Storage Drives

Note

The following sections describe these storage drives in greater detail.

Floppy Drives

A floppy drive, or floppy disk drive, is a storage device that uses removable 3.5-inch floppy disks. These magnetic floppy disks can store 720 KB or 1.44 MB of data. In a computer, the floppy drive is usually configured as the A: drive. The floppy drive can be used to boot the computer if it contains a bootable floppy disk. A 5.25-inch floppy drive is older technology and is seldom used.

The floppy drive is slowly being replaced by cheaper, faster, and larger-capacity storage such as writable CDs, DVDs, and flash drive media.

Optical Drives

An optical drive is a storage device that uses lasers to read data on the optical media. Two types of optical drives:

- Compact disc (CD)
- Digital versatile disc (DVD)

CD and DVD media can be prerecorded (read-only), recordable (write once), or rerecordable (read and write multiple times). CDs have a data storage capacity of approximately 700 MB. DVDs have a data storage capacity of approximately 8.5 GB on one side of the disc.

Several types of optical media exist:

- CD-ROM is CD read-only memory media that is prerecorded.
- CD-R is CD recordable media that can be recorded once.
- CD-RW is CD rewritable media that can be recorded, erased, and rerecorded.
- DVD-ROM is DVD read-only memory media that is prerecorded.
- DVD-RAM is DVD random-access memory media that can be recorded, erased, and rerecorded.
- DVD+/-R is DVD recordable media that can be recorded once.
- DVD+/-RW is DVD rewritable media that can be recorded, erased, and rerecorded.

Flash Drives
A flash drive, also known as a thumb drive, is a removable storage device that connects to a USB port. A flash drive uses a special type of memory that requires no power to maintain the data. These drives can be accessed by the operating system in the same way other types of drives are accessed. The storage capacity of a flash drive varies from a couple of megabytes to 16 gigabytes.

Hard Drives
A hard drive, or hard-disk drive, is a magnetic storage device that is installed inside the computer. The hard drive is used as permanent storage for data. In a computer, the hard drive is usually configured as the C: drive and contains the operating system and applications. The hard drive is usually configured as the first drive in the boot sequence. The storage capacity of a hard drive is measured in billions of bytes, or gigabytes (GB). The speed of a hard drive is measured in revolutions per minute (rpm). Multiple hard drives can be added to increase storage capacity.

Network Drives
A network drive is a connection to a remote computer's storage for access to files, directories, and applications.

1.5   TYPES OF DRIVE INTERFACES
Hard drives and optical drives are manufactured with different interfaces that are used to connect the drive to the computer. When you install a storage drive in a computer, the connection interface on the drive must be the same as the controller on the motherboard. Some common drive interfaces are as follows:

Integrated Drive Electronics (IDE), also called Advanced Technology Attachment (ATA), is an early drive controller interface that connects computers and hard-disk drives. An IDE interface uses a 40-pin connector.

Enhanced Integrated Drive Electronics (EIDE), also called ATA-2, is an updated version of the IDE drive controller interface. EIDE supports hard drives larger than 512 MB, enables Direct Memory Access (DMA) for speed, and uses the AT Attachment Packet Interface (ATAPI) to accommodate optical drives and tape drives on the EIDE bus. An EIDE interface uses a 40-pin connector.

Parallel ATA (PATA) refers to the parallel version of the ATA drive controller interface.

Serial ATA (SATA) refers to the serial version of the ATA drive controller interface. A SATA interface uses a seven-pin connector.

Small Computer System Interface (SCSI) is a drive controller interface that can connect up to 15 drives. SCSI can connect both internal and external drives. A SCSI interface uses a 50-pin, 68-pin, or 80-pin connector.

1.6   ROM AND RAM
ROM and RAM provide memory for a vast amount of computer equipment. They come in different memory sizes and module sizes and have different features. The following sections cover ROM and RAM in greater detail.

ROM
Read-only memory (ROM) chips are located on the motherboard. ROM chips contain instructions that the CPU can access directly. ROM stores basic instructions for booting the computer and loading the operating system. ROM chips retain their contents even when the computer is powered down. The contents cannot be erased, changed, or rewritten by normal means. ROM types include the following:

- Programmable read-only memory (PROM): Information is written to a PROM chip after it is manufactured. A PROM chip cannot be erased or rewritten.

- Erasable programmable read-only memory (EPROM): Information is written to an EPROM chip after it is manufactured. An EPROM chip can be erased with exposure to UV light. Special equipment is required.

- Electrically erasable programmable read-only memory (EEPROM): Information is written to an EEPROM chip after it is manufactured. EEPROM chips are also called flash ROMs. An EEPROM chip can be erased and rewritten without removing the chip from the computer.

Note
ROM is sometimes called firmware. This is misleading, because firmware is actually the software that is stored in a ROM chip.

RAM
Random-Access Memory (RAM) is the temporary storage for data and programs that are being accessed by the CPU. RAM is volatile memory, which means that the contents are erased when the computer is powered off. The more RAM in a computer, the more capacity the computer has to hold and process large programs and files, as well as enhance system performance. The different types of RAM are as follows:

- Dynamic RAM (DRAM) is a memory chip that is used as main memory. DRAM must be constantly refreshed with pulses of electricity to maintain the data stored in the chip.

- Static RAM (SRAM) is a memory chip that is used as cache memory. SRAM is much faster than DRAM and does not have to be refreshed as often.

- Fast Page Mode (FPM) DRAM is memory that supports paging. Paging enables faster access to the data than regular DRAM. Most 486 and Pentium systems from 1995 and earlier use FPM memory.

- Extended Data Out (EDO) RAM is memory that overlaps consecutive data accesses. This speeds up the access time to retrieve data from memory, because the CPU does not have to wait for one data access cycle to end before another data access cycle begins.

- Synchronous DRAM (SDRAM) is DRAM that operates in synchronization with the memory bus. The memory bus is the data path between the CPU and the main memory.

- Double Data Rate (DDR) SDRAM is memory that transfers data twice as fast as SDRAM. DDR SDRAM increases performance by transferring data twice per cycle.

- Double Data Rate 2 (DDR2) SDRAM is faster than DDR-SDRAM memory. DDR2 SDRAM improves performance over DDR SDRAM by decreasing noise and crosstalk between the signal wires.

- RAM Bus DRAM (RDRAM) is a memory chip that was developed to communicate at very high rates of speed. RDRAM chips are not commonly used.

Memory Modules Early computers had RAM installed on the motherboard as individual chips. These individual memory chips, called dual inline package (DIP) chips, were difficult to install and often became loose on the motherboard. To solve this problem, designers soldered the memory chips on a special circuit board called a memory module. The different types of memory modules are as follows:

- Dual Inline Package (DIP) is an individual memory chip. A DIP had dual rows of pins used to attach it to the motherboard.

- Single Inline Memory Module (SIMM) is a small circuit board that holds several memory chips. SIMMs have 30-pin and 72-pin configurations.

- Dual Inline Memory Module (DIMM) is a circuit board that holds SDRAM, DDR SDRAM, and DDR2 SDRAM chips. There are 168-pin SDRAM DIMMs, 184-pin DDR DIMMs, and 240-pin DDR2 DIMMs.

- RAM Bus Inline Memory Module (RIMM) is a circuit board that holds RDRAM chips. A typical RIMM has a 184-pin configuration.

Note

Memory modules can be single-sided or double-sided. Single-sided memory modules contain RAM on only one side of the module. Double-sided memory modules contain RAM on both sides of the module.

1.7   CACHE MEMORY

SRAM is used as cache memory to store the most frequently used data. SRAM gives the processor faster access to the data than retrieving it from the slower DRAM, or main memory.

The three types of cache memory are as follows:

- L1 is internal cache integrated into the CPU.

- L2 is external cache originally mounted on the motherboard near the CPU. L2 cache is now integrated into the CPU.

- L3 is used on some high-end workstations and server CPUs. Error Checking

Memory errors occur when the data is stored incorrectly in the RAM chips. The computer uses different methods to detect and correct data errors in memory. Three different methods of memory error checking are as follows:

- Nonparity does not check for errors in memory.

- Parity contains 8 bits for data and 1 bit for error checking. The error-checking bit is called a parity bit.

- Error Correction Code (ECC) can detect multiple bit errors in memory and correct single bit errors in memory.

1.8 COOLING SYSTEMS

Electronic components generate heat. Heat is caused by the flow of current within the components. Computer components perform better when kept cool. If the heat is not removed, the computer may run slower. If too much heat builds up, computer components can be damaged. Increasing the air flow in the computer case allows more heat to be removed. A case fan is installed in the computer case to make the cooling process more efficient.

Case Fan

In addition to case fans, a heat sink draws heat away from the core of the CPU. A fan on top of the heat sink moves the heat away from the CPU, as shown in Figure 1-6.

Figure 1.6: Case Fan

Other components are also susceptible to heat damage and sometimes are equipped with fans. Video adapter cards produce a great deal of heat. Fans are dedicated to cooling the graphics-processing unit (GPU).

Figure 1.7: CPU Fans

Figure 1.8: Graphics Card Cooling System

Computers with extremely fast CPUs and GPUs may use a water-cooling system. A metal plate is placed over the processor, and water is pumped over the top to collect the heat that the CPU creates. The water is pumped to a radiator to be cooled by the air and then is recirculated.

Adapter Cards
Adapter cards increase a computer's functionality by adding controllers for specific devices or by

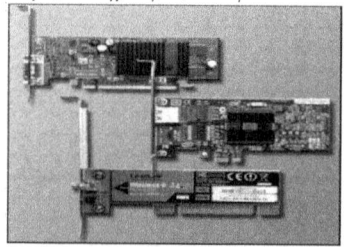

Fig. 1.9: Adapter Cards

Note
Adapter cards are used to expand and customize the computer's capability:

♦   *NIC* connects a computer to a network using a network cable.

♦   **Wireless NIC** connects a computer to a network using radio frequencies.

♦   **Sound adapter** provides audio capability.

1.9   SOUND
The sound device in a computer performs two functions. First, it takes digital information and turns it into sound, outputting the sound through speakers. Second, it takes sound that is input through a microphone or some other audio source and turns it into digital data. To play and record sounds, your sound device needs to connect to a set of speakers and a microphone or more. All PCs have at least two miniature audio jacks: one for a microphone and another for stereo speakers. Better cards provide extra miniature audio jacks for surround sound. Figure 3-22 is a typical onboard soundcard showing six different 1/8-inch jacks. Four of these are for speakers and two are for input (such as microphones). The colour scheme for sound connections is complex, but for now remember one

colourgreen. That's the one you need to connect a standard pair of stereo speakers.

An older sound card may still provide a female 15-pin DB port that enables you to attach an electronic musical instrument interface or add a joystick to your PC.

♦   **Video adapter** provides graphic capability.

♦   **Modem adapter** connects a computer to the Internet using a phone line.

♦   **SCSI adapter** connects SCSI devices, such as hard drives or tape drives, to a computer.

♦   *RAID adapter* connects multiple hard drives to a computer to provide redundancy and to improve performance.

♦   *USB port* connects a computer to peripheral devices.

♦   *Parallel port* connects a computer to peripheral devices.

♦   *Serial port* connects a computer to peripheral devices.

Computers have expansion slots on the motherboard to install adapter cards. The type of adapter card connector must match the expansion slot. A riser card is used in computer systems with the LPX form factor to allow adapter cards to be installed horizontally. The riser card is mainly used in slimline desktop computers. The different types of expansion slots are as follows:

♦   *Industry Standard Architecture (ISA)* is an 8-bit or 16-bit expansion slot. This is older technology and is seldom used.

♦   *Extended Industry Standard Architecture (EISA)* is a 32-bit expansion slot. This is older technology and is seldom used.

♦   *Microchannel Architecture (MCA)* is an IBM-proprietary 32-bit expansion slot. This is older technology and is seldom used.

♦   *Peripheral Component Interconnect (PCI)* is a 32-bit or 64-bit expansion slot. PCI is the standard slot currently used in most computers.

♦   *Advanced Graphics Port (AGP)* is a 32-bit expansion slot. AGP is designed for video adapters.

♦   *PCI-Express* is a serial bus expansion slot. PCI-Express is backward-compatible with PCI slots. PCI-Express has x1, x4, x8, x16 slots.

1.10   INTERNAL CABLES

Drives require both a power cable and a data cable. A power supply has a SATA power connector for SATA drives, a Molex power connector for PATA drives, and a Berg four-pin connector for floppy drives. The buttons and the LED lights on the front of the case connect to the motherboard with the front panel cables. Figure 1-10 shows some examples of internal PC cables.

Data cables connect drives to the drive controller, which is located on an adapter card or the motherboard. Some common types of data cables are as follows:

♦   **Floppy disk drive (FDD)** data cable has up to two 34-pin drive connectors and one 34-pin connector for the drive controller.

♦   **PATA (IDE)** data cable has 40 conductors, up to two 40-pin connectors for drives, and one 40-pin connector for the drive controller.

♦   **PATA (EIDE)** data cable has 80 conductors, up to two 40-pin connectors for drives, and one 40-pin connector for the drive controller.

♦   **SATA** data cable has seven conductors, one keyed connector for the drive, and one keyed connector the drive controller.

♦   **SCSI** data cable: Three types of SCSI data cables exist:

♦   A narrow SCSI data cable has 50 conductors, up to seven 50-pin connectors for drives, and one 50-pin connector for the drive controller, also called the host adapter.

♦   A wide SCSI data cable has 68 conductors, up to 15 68-pin connectors for drives, and one 68-pin connector for the host adapter.

♦   An Alt-4 SCSI data cable has 80 conductors, up to 15 80-pin connectors for drives, and one 80-pin connector for the host adapter.

SATA Data Cable, FDD Data Cable and PATA Data Cable

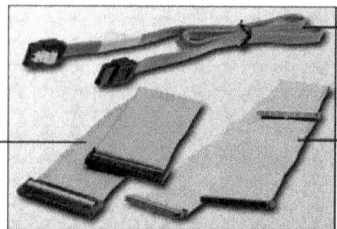

Figure 1.10:   Internal PC Cables

Note

A coloured stripe on a cable identifies Pin 1 on the cable. When installing a data cable, always ensure that Pin 1 on the cable aligns with Pin 1 on the drive or drive controller. Some cables may be keyed; therefore, they can be connected only one way to the drive and drive controller.

Ports and Cables

I/O ports on a computer connect peripheral devices, such as printers, scanners, and portable drives. The following ports and cables are commonly used:

♦   Serial

♦   USB

♦   FireWire

♦   Parallel

♦   SCSI

♦   Network

♦   PS/2

♦   Audio

♦   Video

The following sections explain port and cable topics in greater detail.

Serial Ports and Cables

A serial port can be either a DB-9, as shown in Figure 1-11, or a DB-25 male connector.

Serial ports transmit 1 bit of data at a time. To connect a serial device, such as a modem or printer, a serial cable must be used. A serial cable has a maximum length of 50 feet (15.2 m).

Figure 1.11:   Serial Ports and Cables

USB Ports and Cables

The Universal Serial Bus (USB) is a standard interface that connects peripheral devices to a computer. It was originally designed to replace serial and parallel connections. USB devices are hot-swappable, which means that users can connect and disconnect the devices while the computer is powered on. USB connections can be found on computers, cameras, printers, scanners, storage devices, and many other electronic devices. A USB hub is used to connect multiple USB devices. A single USB port in a computer can support up to 127 separate devices with the use of multiple USB hubs. Some devices can also be powered through the USB port, eliminating the need for an external

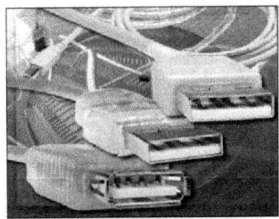

Figure 1.12:   USB Connectors

USB 1.1 allowed transmission rates of up to 12 Mbps in full-speed mode and 1.5 Mbps in low-speed mode. USB 2.0 allows transmission speeds up to 480 Mbps. USB devices can only transfer data up to the maximum speed allowed by the specific port.

FireWire Ports and Cables

FireWire is a high-speed, hot-swappable interface that connects peripheral devices to a computer. A single FireWire port in a computer can support up to 63 devices. Some devices can also be powered through the FireWire port, eliminating the need for an external power source. FireWire uses the IEEE 1394 standard and is also known as i.Link. The IEEE 1394a standard supports data rates up to 400 Mbps and cable lengths up to 15 feet (4.5 m). This standard uses a six-pin connector or a four-pin connector. The IEEE 1394b standard supports data rates in excess of 800 Mbps and uses a nine-pin connector.

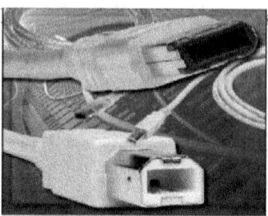

Figure 1.13: FireWire Connectors

Parallel Ports and Cables

A parallel port on a computer is a standard Type A DB-25 female connector. The parallel connector on a printer is a standard Type B 36-pin Centronics connector. Some newer printers may use a Type C high-density 36-pin connector. Parallel ports can transmit 8 bits of data at a time and use the IEEE 1284 standard. To connect a parallel device, such as a printer, a parallel cable must be used. A

14, has a maximum length of 15 feet (4.5 m).

Figure 1.14: Parallel Cable

SCSI Ports and Cables

A SCSI port can transmit data at rates in excess of 320 Mbps and can support up to 15 devices. If a single SCSI device is connected to a SCSI port, the cable can be up to 80 feet (24.4 m) in length. If multiple SCSI devices are connected to a SCSI port, the cable can be up to 40 (12.2 m) feet in length. A SCSI port on a computer can be one of three different types:

♦   DB-25 female connector
♦   High-density 50-pin female connector

♦ High-density 68-pin female connector

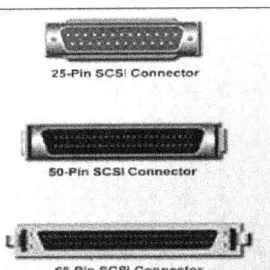

25-Pin SCSI Connector

50-Pin SCSI Connector

68-Pin SCSI Connector

Figure 1.15: SCSI Connectors

Note
SCSI devices must be terminated at the endpoints of the SCSI chain. Check the device manual for termination procedures.

Caution
Some SCSI connectors resemble parallel connectors. Be careful not to connect the cable to the wrong port. The voltage used in the SCSI format may damage the parallel interface. SCSI connectors should be clearly labeled.

Network Ports and Cables
A network port, also called an RJ-45 port, connects a computer to a network. The connection speed depends on the type of network port. Standard Ethernet can transmit up to 10Mbps, Fast Ethernet can transmit up to 100 Mbps, and Gigabit Ethernet can transmit up to 1000 Mbps. The maximum length of network cable is 328 feet (100 ma network connector.

Figure 1.16: Network Connector

PS/2 Ports
A *PS/2 port* connects a keyboard or mouse to a computer. The PS/2 port is a six-pin mini-DIN female connector. The connectors for the keyboard and mouse are often coloured differently, as shown in Figure 1.17. If the ports are not colour-coded, look for a small figure of a mouse or keyboard next to each port.

Figure 1.17: PS/2 Ports

Audio Ports

An audio port connects audio devices to the computer. The following audio ports are commonly used, as shown in Figure 1-18:

♦ **Line In** connects to an external source, such as a stereo system.

♦ **Microphone In** connects to a microphone.

♦ **Line Out** connects to speakers or headphones.

♦ **Auxiliary In** is an additional line in.

♦ **Game port/MIDI** connects to a joystick or MIDI-interfaced device.

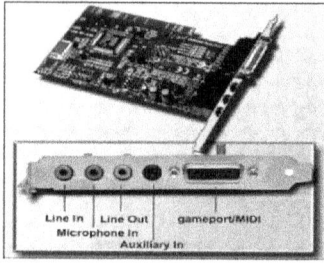

Figure 1.18: Audio Ports

Video Ports and Connectors

A video port connects a monitor cable to a computer. Several video port and connector types exist:

♦ *Video Graphics Array (VGA)* has a three-row 15-pin female connector and provides analog output to a monitor.

♦ *Digital Visual Interface (DVI)* has a 24-pin female connector or a 29-pin female connector and provides compressed digital output to a monitor. DVI-I provides both analog and digital signals. DVI-D provides digital signals only.

♦ *High-Definition Multimedia Interface (HDMI)* has a 19-pin connector and provides digital video and digital audio signals.

♦   *S-Video* has a four-pin connector and provides analog video signals.

♦   *Component/RGB* has three shielded cables (red, green, and blue) with RCA jacks and

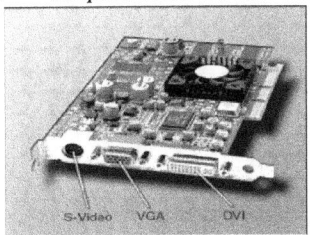

Figure 1.19: Shows the Video Ports on a Video Card

Input Devices

An input device is used to enter data or instructions into a computer. Here are some examples of input devices:

-   Mouse and keyboard
-   Digital camera and digital video camera
-   Biometric authentication device
-   Touch screen
-   Scanner

The mouse and keyboard are the two most commonly used input devices. The mouse is used to navigate the graphical user interface (GUI). The keyboard is used to enter text commands that control the computer.

Digital cameras and digital video cameras, shown in Figure 1-20, create images that can be stored on magnetic media. The image is stored as a file that can be displayed, printed, or altered.

Figure 1.20: Digital Cameras

Biometric identification uses features that are unique to an individual user, such as: fingerprints, voice recognition, or a retinal scan. When combined with ordinary usernames, biometrics guarantees that the authorized person is accessing the data.

Figure 1.21 shows a laptop that has a built-in fingerprint scanner

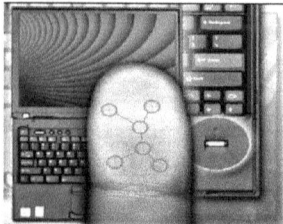

Figure 1.21: Fingerprint Scanner

A touch screen has a pressure-sensitive transparent panel. The computer receives instructions specific to the place on the screen that the user touches.

A scanner digitizes an image or document. The digitization of the image is stored as a file that can be displayed, printed, or altered. A bar code reader is a type of scanner that reads Universal Product Code (UPC) bar codes. It is widely used for pricing and inventory information.

Identification of Output Devices

An output device is used to present information to the user from a computer. Here are some examples of output devices:

-    Printers, scanners, and fax machines
-    Monitors and projectors
-    Speakers and headphones

1.11 PRINTERS, SCANNERS, AND PHOTOCOPYING MACHINES

Printers are output devices that create hard copies of computer files. Some printers specialize in particular applications, such as printing colour photographs. Other all-in-one-type printers, such as the one shown in Figure 1.22, are designed to provide multiple services such as printing, scanning, and copier functions.

Figure 1.22: All-in-One Printer

Monitors and Projectors

Monitors and projectors are primary output devices for a computer. Figure 1.23 shows different types of monitors.

Figure 1.23: Monitors and Projectors
Types of Monitors
♦ DLP Projector
♦ LCD CRT

The most important difference between these monitor types is the technology used to create an image:

♦ **CRT**: Cathode ray tube monitors are the most common monitor type. Red, green, and blue electron beams move back and forth across the phosphorous-coated screen. The phosphor glows when struck by the electron beam. Areas not struck by the electron beam do not glow.

♦ **LCD**: Liquid crystal display is commonly used in laptops and some projectors. It consists of two polarizing filters with a liquid crystal solution between them. An electronic current aligns the crystals so that light can either pass through or not pass through. The effect of light passing through in certain areas and not in others is what creates the image. LCD comes in two forms active matrix and passive matrix. Active matrix is sometimes called thin film transistor (TFT). TFT allows each pixel to be controlled, which creates very sharp colour images. Passive matrix is less expensive than active matrix but does not provide the same level of image control. LCD Monitors are becoming the most common type of computer

Figure 1.24: Speakers and Headphones

Speakers and headphones, shown in Figure 1.24, are output devices for audio signals. Most computers have audio support either integrated into the motherboard or on an adapter card. Audio support includes ports that allow input and output of audio signals. The audio card has an amplifier to power headphones and external speakers.
Speakers and Headphones

Explain System Resources and Their Purposes
System resources are used for communication between the CPU and other components in a

computer. The three common system resources are

♦   Interrupt requests (IRQ)

♦   I/O port addresses

♦   Direct Memory Access (DMA)

The following sections describe these system resources in greater detail.

Interrupt Requests

Computer components use ***interrupt requests (IRQ)*** to request information from the CPU. The IRQ travels along a wire on the motherboard to the CPU. When the CPU receives an interrupt request, it determines how to fulfill this request. The priority of the request is determined by the IRQ number assigned to that computer component. Older computers had only eight IRQs to assign to devices. Newer computers have 16 IRQs, which are numbered 0 to 15, each component in the computer must be assigned a unique IRQ. IRQ conflicts can cause components to stop functioning and even cause the computer to crash. With the numerous components that can be installed in a computer, it is difficult to assign a unique IRQ to every component. Today, most IRQ numbers are assigned automatically with "plug-and-play" operating systems and the implementation of PCI slots, USB ports, and FireWire ports.

Input/Output (I/O) Port Addresses

Input/output (I/O) Port Addresses are used to communicate between devices and software. The I/O port address is used to send and receive data for a component. As with IRQs, each component has a unique I/O port assigned. A computer has 65,535 I/O ports, and they are referenced by a hexadecimal address in the range of 0000h to FFFFh. Table 1-11 is a chart of common I/O ports.

Direct Memory Access

High-speed devices use ***Direct Memory Access (DMA)*** channels to communicate directly with the main memory. These channels allow the device to bypass interaction with the CPU and directly store information in memory and retrieve it. Only certain devices can be assigned a DMA channel, such as SCSI host adapters and sound cards. Older computers had only four DMA channels to assign to components.

REVISION QUESTIONS

1.   What is the purpose of a heat sink installed on a processor?
     A. To cool the processor   B. To set the processor voltage
     C. To set the processor speed   D. To ground the processor
2.   Which type of memory transfers data twice as fast as SDRAM and increases performance by transferring data twice per cycle?
     A. D-SDRAM   B. ROM   C. DDR-SDRAM   D. DRAM2
3.   How many FireWire devices can a single FireWire port support?
     A. 12   B. 63   C. 127   D. 54   E. 25   F. 32
4.   Which type of video connector has a 24-pin or 29-pin female connector and provides compressed digital output to a monitor?
     A. VGA   B. RCA   C. HDMI   D. DVI   E. AAV
5.   How many universal serial bus (USB) devices can be connected to a USB port?
     A. 64   B. 127   C. 256   D. 128
6.   What is the maximum data speed of high-speed USB 2.0?
     A. 480 Gbps   B. 12 Mbps   C. 380 Mbps

CHAPTER TWO

COMPUTER ASSEMBLING

2.1 INTRODUCTION

Assembling computers is a large part of a technician's job. As a technician, you will need to work in a logical, methodical manner when working with computer components. As with any learned trade, your computer assembly skills will improve dramatically with practice.

2.2 OPEN THE CASE

Computer cases are produced in a variety of form factors. Form factors refer to the `size and shape of the case. Prepare the workspace before opening the computer case. There should be adequate lighting, good ventilation, and a comfortable room temperature. The workbench or table should be accessible from all sides. Avoid cluttering the surface of the workbench or table with tools and computer components. An antistatic mat on the table will help prevent physical and *electrostatic discharge* (ESD) damage to equipment. Small containers can be used to hold screws and other parts as you remove them.

There are different methods of opening cases. To learn how to open a particular computer case, consult the user manual or manufacturer's website. Most computer cases are opened in one of the following ways:

♦   The case's top and side panels can be removed.
♦   The computer case cover can be removed as one piece.
♦   The top of the case may need to be removed before the side panels can be removed.

2.3 INSTALLATION - THE POWER SUPPLY

A technician may be required to replace or install a *power supply*, as shown in Figure 2.1. Most power supplies can fit only one way in the computer case. Usually, three or four screws attach the power supply to the case. Power supplies have fans that can vibrate and loosen screws that are not secured. When installing a power supply, make sure that all the screws are used and that they are properly tightened.

These are the power supply installation steps:

Step 1:   Insert the power supply into the case.

Step 2:   Align the holes in the power supply with the holes in the case.

Step 3:   Secure the power supply to the case using the proper screws.

Figure 2.1: Power Supply

2.4   ATTACH THE COMPONENTS TO THE MOTHERBOARD AND INSTALLATION

This section details the steps to install components on the ***motherboard*** and then install the motherboard into the computer case.

After completing this section, you will meet these objectives:
-   Install a CPU and a heat sink/fan assembly.
-   Install the RAM.
-   Install the motherboard.

2.5   INSTALLATION OF CPU

The ***Central Processing Unit (CPU)*** and the ***heat sink/fan*** assembly may be installed on the motherboard before the motherboard is placed in the computer case.

Figure 2.2 shows a close-up view of the CPU and the motherboard. The CPU and motherboard are sensitive to electrostatic discharge. When handling a CPU and motherboard, make sure that you place them on a grounded antistatic mat. You should wear an antistatic wrist strap while working with these components.

Figure 2.2:   CPU and Motherboard

Caution
When handling a CPU, do not touch the CPU contacts at any time. The CPU is secured to the socket on the motherboard with a locking assembly. CPU sockets today are ***zero insertion force (ZIF) sockets***. You should be familiar with the locking assembly before attempting to install a CPU into the socket on the motherboard.

Thermal compound helps keep the CPU cool. Figure 3.3 shows thermal compound being applied to the CPU. When you are installing a used CPU, clean the CPU and the base of the heat sink with *isopropylalcohol*. Doing this removes all traces of old thermal compound. The surfaces are now ready for a new layer of thermal compound. Follow all manufacturer recommendations about

Figure 2.3: Thermal Compound on the CPU

Figure 2.4 shows the heat sink/fan assembly. It is a two-part cooling device. The heat sink draws heat away from the CPU, and the fan moves the heat away from the heat sink. The heat sink/fan assembly usually has a three-pin power connector.

Figure 2.4: Heat Sink/Fan Assembly on the Motherboard

Follow these instructions for CPU and heat sink/fan assembly installation:

Step 1: Align the CPU so that the Connection 1 indicator is lined up with Pin 1 on the CPU socket. Doing this ensures that the orientation notches on the CPU are aligned with the orientation keys on the CPU socket.

Step 2: Place the CPU gently into the socket.

How To

Step 3: Close the CPU load plate and secure it in place by closing the load lever and moving it under the load lever retention tab.

Step 4: Carefully apply a small amount of thermal compound to the CPU, and spread it evenly. Follow the application instructions provided by the manufacturer.

Step 5: Align the heat sink/fan assembly retainers with the holes on the motherboard.

Step 6: Place the heat sink/fan assembly onto the CPU socket, being careful not to pinch the CPU fan wires.

Step 7: Tighten the heat sink/fan assembly retainers to secure the assembly in place.

Step 8: Connect the heat sink/fan assembly power cable to the header on the motherboard.

Install the RAM

Like the CPU and the heat sink/fan assembly, ***random-access memory (RAM)*** is installed in the motherboard before the motherboard is secured in the computer case. Before you install a memory module, consult the motherboard documentation or website of the manufacturer to ensure that the RAM is compatible with the motherboard. RAM provides temporary data storage for the CPU while the computer is operating.

RAM is ***volatile memory***, which means that its contents are lost when the computer is shut down. Typically, more RAM enhances your computer's performance. Follow these steps for RAM installation:

Step 1:   Align the notches on the RAM module to the keys in the slot, and press down until the side tabs click into place.

Step 2:   Make sure that the side tabs have locked the RAM module. Visually check for exposed contacts. Repeat these steps for additional RAM modules.

2.6   INSTALLATION OF THE MOTHERBOARD

The motherboard is now ready to install in the computer case. Plastic and metal standoffs are used to mount the motherboard and to prevent it from touching the metal portions of the case. You should install only the standoffs that align with the holes in the motherboard. Installing any additional standoffs may prevent the motherboard from being seated properly in the computer case.

How To

Follow these steps for motherboard installation:

Step 1:   Install standoffs in the computer case.
Step 2:   Align the I/O connectors on the back of the motherboard with the openings in the back of the case.
Step 3:   Align the screw holes of the motherboard with the standoffs.
Step 4:   Insert all the motherboard screws.
Step 5:   Tighten all the motherboard screws.

Install the Motherboard

In this lab you install the CPU, heat sink/fan assembly, RAM, and motherboard. You may perform this lab now or wait until the end of the chapter.

Install Internal Drives

Drives that are installed in internal bays are called internal drives. A ***hard disk drive (HDD)*** is an example of an internal drive.

Follow these steps for HDD installation:
Step 1:   Position the HDD so that it aligns with the 3.5-inch drive bay.
Step 2:   Insert the HDD into the drive bay so that the screw holes in the drive line up with the screw holes in the case.
Step 3:   Secure the HDD to the case using the proper screws.
How To

Install Drives in External Bays

Drives, such as optical drives and floppy drives, are installed in drive bays that are accessed from the front of the case. Optical drives and floppy drives store data on removable media. Drives in external bays let you access the media without opening the case.

After completing this section, you will meet these objectives:
- Install the optical drive.
- Install the floppy drive.

Install the Optical Drive

An *optical drive* is a storage device that reads and writes information to CDs and DVDs. A *Molex power connector* provides the optical drive with power from the power supply. A PATA cable connects the optical drive to the motherboard.

Follow these steps for optical drive installation:

Step 1:   Position the optical drive so that it aligns with the 5.25-inch drive bay.

Step 2:   Insert the optical drive into the drive bay so that the optical drive screw holes align with the screw holes in the case.

Step 3:   Secure the optical drive to the case using the proper screws.

Install the Floppy Drive

A *floppy disk drive (FDD)* is a storage device that reads and writes information to a floppy data cable connects the FDD to the motherboard. A floppy disk drive fits into the 3.5-inch bay on the front of the computer case, as shown in Figure 2.5. Follow these steps for FDD installation:

Step 1:   Position the FDD so that it aligns with the 3.5-inch drive bay.

Step 2:   Insert the FDD into the drive bay so that the FDD screw holes align with thescrew holes in the case.

Step 3:   Secure the FDD to the case using the proper screws.

How To

Figure 2.5: Floppy Drive Installed

Install the Drives
In this lab you install the hard drive, optical drive, and floppy drive

Install Adapter Cards
Adapter cards are installed to add functionality to a computer. Adapter cards must be compatible with the expansion slot. This section focuses on the installation of three types of adapter cards:

♦   PCIe x1 NIC
♦   PCI wireless NIC
♦   PCIe x16 video adapter card

After completing this section, you will meet these objectives:
♦   Install the NIC.
♦   Install the wireless NIC.
♦   Install the video adapter card.

Install the NIC
A *Network Interface Card (NIC)* enables a computer to connect to a network. NICs use PCI and PCIe expansion slots on the motherboard, as shown in Figure 2.6.

Figure 2.6: Network Interface Card

PC Hardware Essentials: Practical Guide
Follow these steps for NIC installation:

Step 1:   Align the NIC to the appropriate expansion slot on the motherboard.

Step 2:   Press down gently on the NIC until the card is fully seated.

Step 3:   Secure the NIC PC mounting bracket to the case with the appropriate screw.

Install the Wireless NIC
A wireless NIC, as shown in Figure 2.7, enables a computer to connect to a wireless network. Wireless NICs use PCI and PCIe expansion slots on the motherboard. Some wireless NICs are installed externally with a USB connector.

Follow these steps for wireless NIC installation:
Step 1:   Align the wireless NIC to the appropriate expansion slot on the motherboard.
Step 2:   Press down gently on the wireless NIC until the card is fully seated.

Step 3:   Secure the wireless NIC PC mounting bracket to the case with the appropriate screw.

How To

Figure 2.7: Wireless NIC

Install the Video Adapter Card
A *video adapter card*, shown in Figure 2.8, is the interface between a computer and a display monitor. An upgraded video adapter card can provide better graphics capabilities for games and graphic programs. Video adapter cards use PCI, AGP, and PCIe expansion slots on the motherboard.

Figure 2.8: Video Adapter Card

Follow these steps for video adapter card installation:

Step 1:   Align the video adapter card to the appropriate expansion slot on the motherboard.
Step 2:   Press down gently on the video adapter card until the card is fully seated.
Step 3:   Secure the video adapter card PC mounting bracket to the case with the appropriate screw.

Connect All Internal Cables
Power cables are used to distribute electricity from the power supply to the motherboard and other components. Data cables transmit data between the motherboard and storage devices, such as hard drives. Additional cables connect the buttons and link lights on the front of the computer case to the motherboard.

After completing this section, you will meet these objectives:
-       Connect the power cables.
-       Connect the data cables.
Connect the Power Cables
This section deals with the following:

♦   Motherboard power connections

♦   SATA power connectors

♦   Molex power connectors

♦   Berg power connectors

♦   Motherboard Power Connections

Just like other components, motherboards require power to operate. The ***Advanced Technology Extended (ATX)*** main power connector has either 20 or 24 pins. The power supply may also have a four-pin or six-pin auxiliary (AUX) power connector that connects to the motherboard. A 20-pin connector will work in a motherboard with a 24-pin socket.

Follow these steps for motherboard power cable installation:

Step 1:   Align the 20-pin ATX power connector to the socket on the motherboard.

Step 2:   Gently press down on the connector until the clip clicks into place.

Step 3:   Align the four-pin AUX power connector to the socket on the motherboard.

Step 4:   Gently press down on the connector until the clip clicks into place.

2.7   SATA POWER CONNECTORS

Serial Advanced Technology Attachment (SATA) power connectors use a 15-pin connector. SATA power connectors are used to connect to hard disk drives, optical drives, or any devices that have a SATA power socket.

Molex Power Connectors Hard disk drives and optical drives that do not have SATA power sockets use a Molex power connector.

Caution
Do not use a Molex connector and a SATA power connector on the same drive at the same time.

Berg Power Connectors
The four-pin Berg power connector supplies power to a floppy drive.

Follow these steps for power connector installation:

Step 1:   Plug the SATA power connector into the HDD.

Step 2:   Plug the Molex power connector into the optical drive.

Step 3:   Plug the four-pin Berg power connector into the FDD.

Step 4:   Connect the three-pin fan power connector into the appropriate fan header on the motherboard according to the motherboard manual.

Step 5:   Plug the additional cables from the case into the appropriate connectors according to the motherboard manual.

Connect the Data Cables
Drives connect to the motherboard using data cables. The drive being connected determines the type of data cable used. The types of data cables are PATA, SATA, and floppy drive.

How To
PATA Data Cables

The ***Parallel Advanced Technologies Attachment (PATA) Cable*** is sometimes called a ribbon cable because it is wide and flat. The PATA cable can have either 40 or 80 conductors. A PATA cable usually has three 40-pin connectors. One connector at the end of the cable connects to the motherboard. The other two connectors connect to drives. The end of the PATA cable is keyed and can be inserted only one way.

A stripe on the data cable denotes pin 1. Plug the PATA cable into the drive with the pin 1 indicator on the cable aligned to the pin 1 indicator on the drive connector. The pin 1 indicator on the drive connector is usually closest to the power connector on the drive. Many motherboards have two PATA drive controllers, which provide support for a maximum of four PATA drives.

SATA Data Cables
The *Serial Advanced Technology Attachment (SATA) Data Cable* has a seven-pin connector. One end of the cable is connected to the motherboard. The other end is connected to any drive that has a SATA data connector.

Floppy Data Cables
The floppy drive data cable has a 34-pin connector. Like the PATA data cable, the floppy drive data cable has a stripe to denote the location of pin 1. A floppy drive data cable usually has three 34-pin connectors. One connector at the end of the cable connects to the motherboard. The other two connectors connect to drives. If multiple floppy drives are installed, the A: drive connects to the end connector after the twist in the cable.

The B: drive connects to the middle connector.
Plug the floppy drive data cable into the drive with the pin 1 indicator on the cable aligned to the pin 1 indicator on the drive connector. Motherboards have one floppy drive controller, which provides support for a maximum of two floppy drives.

Note
If pin 1 on the floppy drive data cable is not aligned with pin 1 on the drive connector, the floppy drive will not function. This misalignment will not damage the drive, but the drive activity light will display continuously. To fix this problem, turn off the computer and reconnect the data cable so that pin 1 on the cable and pin 1 on the connector are aligned. Reboot the computer.

Data Cable Installation
Follow these steps for data cable installation:

Step 1:   Plug the motherboard end of the PATA cable into the motherboard socket.
Step 2:   Plug the connector at the far end of the PATA cable into the optical drive.
Step 3:   Plug one end of the SATA cable into the motherboard socket.
Step 4:   Plug the other end of the SATA cable into the HDD.
Step 5:   Plug the motherboard end of the FDD cable into the motherboard socket.
Step 6:   Plug the connector at the far end of the FDD cable into the floppy drive.

Install Internal Cables
Reattach the Side Panels and Connect External Cables to the Computer
Now that all the internal components have been installed and connected to the motherboard and power supply, the side panels are reattached to the computer case. The next step is to connect the cables for all computer peripherals and the power cable.

After completing this section, you will meet these objectives:
♦   Reattach the side panels to the case.
♦   Connect external cables to the computer.

Reattach the Side Panels to the Case

Most computer cases have two panels, one on each side. Some computer cases have one three-sided cover that slides over the case frame. As soon as the cover is in place, make sure that it is secured at all screw locations. Some computer cases use screws that are inserted with a screwdriver. Other cases have knob-type screws that can be tightened by hand. If you are unsure how to remove or replace the computer case, refer to the documentation or the manufacturer's website for more information.

Caution

Handle case parts with care. Some computer case covers have sharp or jagged edges.

Connect External Cables to the Computer

After the case panels have been reattached, connect the cables to the back of the computer.

Here are some common external cable connections:
♦   Monitor
♦   Keyboard
♦   Mouse
♦   USB
♦   Ethernet
♦   Power

When attaching cables, ensure that they are connected to the correct locations on the computer. For example, some mouse and keyboard cables use the same type of PS/2 connector.

Caution

When attaching cables, never force a connection.

Note

Plug in the power cable after you have connected all other cables.

Follow these steps for external cable installation:
Step 1:   Attach the monitor cable to the video port.
Step 2:   Secure the cable by tightening the screws on the connector.
Step 3:   Plug the keyboard cable into the PS/2 keyboard port.
Step 4:   Plug the mouse cable into the PS/2 mouse port.
Step 5:   Plug the USB cable into a USB port.
Step 6:   Plug the network cable into the network port.
Step 7:   Connect the wireless antenna to the antenna connector.
Step 8:   Plug the power cable into the power supply.

Figure 2.9 shows all the external cables plugged into the back of the computer.

How To

Figure 3.9: All External Cables Plugged into the Back
Lab 3.8.2: Complete the Computer Assembly
In this lab you reattach the case and connect the external cables to complete the computer Assembly.

Boot the Computer for the First Time
When the computer is booted, the *basic input/output system (BIOS)* performs a check of all the internal components, as shown in Figure 2.10. This check is called a power-on self test (POST). After completing this section, you will meet these objectives:

-     Identify beep codes.
-     Describe the BIOS setup.

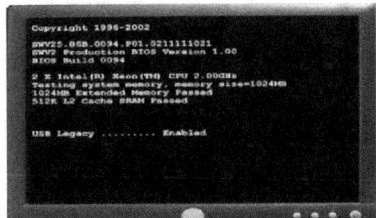

Figure 2.10: POST Screen Shot

Beep Codes
POST checks to see that all the hardware in the computer is operating correctly. If a device is malfunctioning, an error or *beep code* alerts the technician that a problem has occurred. Typically, a single beep denotes that the computer is functioning properly. If a hardware problem exists, the computer may emit a series of beeps. Each BIOS manufacturer uses different codes to indicate hardware problems. Table 2.1 is a sample chart of beep codes. The beep codes for your computer may be different. Consult the motherboard documentation to view beep codes for your computer.

Beep Code	Meaning	Cause
1 beep (no video)	Memory refresh failure	Bad memory
2 beeps	Memory parity error	Bad memory
3 beeps	Base 64K memory failure	Bad memory
4 beeps	Timer not operational	Bad motherboard
5 beeps	Processor error	Bad processor
6 beeps	8042 gate A20 failure	Bad CPU or motherboard
7 beeps	Processor exception	Bad processor
8 beeps	Video memory error	Bad video card or memory

Table 2.1: Sample Beep Codes

Describe the BIOS Setup

The BIOS contains a setup program used to configure settings for hardware devices. The configuration data is saved to a special memory chip called a ***complementary metal-oxide semiconductor (CMOS)***. CMOS is maintained by the battery in the computer. If this battery dies, all BIOS setup configuration data is lost. If this occurs, replace the battery and reconfigure the BIOS settings.

To enter the BIOS setup program, you must press the proper key or key sequence during POST. Most computers use the Delete key. Your computer may use another key or combination of keys, as specified during the boot process.

Figure 2.11: BIOS Setup Screen Shot

Beep Code Meaning Cause

Here are some common BIOS setup menu options:

♦   **Main:** System time, date, HDD type, and so on
♦   **Advanced:** Infrared port settings, parallel port settings, and so on
♦   **Security:** Password settings for the setup utility
♦   **Others:** Low-battery alarm, system beep, and so on
♦   **Boot:** The computer's boot order
♦   **Exit:** Exits the setup utility

Lab 3.9.2: Boot the Computer

Summary

This chapter detailed the steps used to assemble a computer and boot the system for the first time. These are some important points to remember:

♦   Computer cases come in a variety of sizes and configurations. Many of the computer's components must match the case's form factor.

♦   The CPU is installed on the motherboard with a heat sink/fan assembly.

♦   RAM is installed in RAM slots found on the motherboard.

♦   Adapter cards are installed in PCI and PCIe expansion slots found on the motherboard.

♦   Hard disk drives are installed in 3.5-inch drive bays located inside the case.

♦   Optical drives are installed in 5.25-inch drive bays that can be accessed from outside the case.

♦   Floppy drives are installed in 3.5-inch drive bays that can be accessed from outside the case.

♦   Power supply cables are connected to all drives and the motherboard.

♦   Internal data cables transfer data to all drives.

♦   External cables connect peripheral devices to the computer.

♦   Beep codes signify when hardware malfunctions.

♦   The BIOS setup program is used to display information about the computer components and allows the user to change system settings.

REVISION QUESTIONS

1. A technician is installing additional memory in a computer. How can the technician guarantee that the memory is correctly aligned?
    A. All memory and motherboard slots are colour-coded, with one red end and one blue end.
    B. A notch in the memory module should be aligned with a notch in the memory slot.
    C. The arrows on the memory module should be aligned with the arrows on the motherboard slot.
    D. The label on the memory module should always face the CPU.

2. When mounting a motherboard in a computer case, what does the technician use to prevent the motherboard from touching the bottom of the case?
    A. Silicon spray   B. Ground-fault isolators
    C. Grounding straps   D. Standoffs

3. A technician is installing a new power supply in a computer. Which type of power connector should be used to connect to a CD-ROM?
    A. 20-pin ATX connector   B. Mini-Molex   C. Molex   D. Berg

4. A technician is installing a new power supply in a computer. Which type of power connector should be used to connect to an ATX motherboard?
    A. Berg   B. 20-pin connector   C. Molex   D. Mini-Molex

5. Which two connectors are used to connect external peripherals?
    A. EIDE   B. PS/2   C. Molex   D. PATA   E. USB

6. When installing adapter cards in a computer, how should a technician properly secure the card?
    A. Install the card, and secure it to the case with a screw. PC Hardware and Software Essentials: Guide

CHAPTER THREE

MICROSOFT WINDOWS

3.1 INTRODUCTION

In this chapter, you will learn how to:

♦ Identify the operating system folders of Windows 2000, XP, Vista, Window 7 and Window 8.
♦ Explain the Windows interface
♦ Describe the utilities in Windows essential to techs
♦ Relate the history of Microsoft Windows

As a tech, you need to understand Windows at a level beyond that of regular users. This chapter introduces you to some of the more powerful aspects of Windows, such as NTFS and the Registry. Not only must techs run through the standard Windows features that everyone uses every day (Start button, Recycle Bin, and so on), they must also be comfortable drilling down underneath that user-friendly surface to get their hands a little dirty.

This chapter begins by introducing and organizing the many variations of Windows on the market today and helping you appreciate the difference between, for example, Windows XP Home and Windows Vista Ultimate. The chapter then takes you through the Windows interface in detail. The third section looks more closely at the techie aspects of Windows, including the structure of the operating system (OS). The fourth section provides an overview of the many utilities for techs available in Windows.

3.2 A BRIEF HISTORY OF MICROSOFT WINDOWS

Many users think of Windows as a monolithic thing, as *the* operating system (OS) for the PC (as opposed to the Macintosh), but as a tech you need to understand that Microsoft produces many varieties of the OS, each with specific tools, utilities, file structures, and interfaces. And you need to be able to navigate through any modern version of Window

Microsoft currently supports seven families of Windows, of which three concern the technician: Windows 2000, Windows XP, and Windows Vista. (I'll cover the other four families of Windows in the "Beyond A+" section of this chapter.) Within each of these familiesmy word, not Microsoft'sWindows comes in multiple versions. Here's the list for the top three:

Windows Family Versions (32-bit) Versions (64-bit)

Windows 2000 ? Windows 2000 Professional

♦ Windows 2000 Server
♦ Nothing widely available
♦ Windows XP ? Windows XP Home
♦ Windows XP Professional

♦   Windows Media Centre

♦   Windows XP Tablet1

♦   Windows XP 64-bit version

♦   Windows XP Professional x64 Edition Windows Vista2

♦   Windows Vista Home Basic

♦   Windows Vista Home Premium

♦   Windows Vista Business

♦   Windows Vista Ultimate

♦   Windows Vista Home Basic

♦   Windows Vista Home Premium

♦   Windows Vista Business

♦   Windows Vista Ultimate

Microsoft has released two other versions of Windows Vista: Starter Edition and Enterprise. Vista Starter Edition is a simplified version of the operating system designed for the developing world and is not sold in developed countries. Vista Enterprise is a version of Vista Business designed for large-volume customers and is only sold to Microsoft's enterprise-level customers.

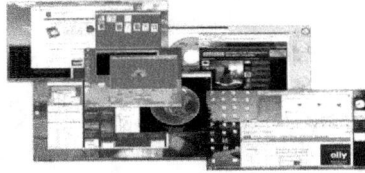

Figure 3.1: Lots of Windows!

The problem of variety is compounded the minute you start working with older Computers or talking with users or techs who've been in computers for a few years. You'll hear about Windows 95, for example, or Windows Me, or even Windows 3.x. Huh? What are these versions (Figure 3.1)? How do they fit in the picture?

3.3   UNDERSTANDING MICROSOFT WINDOWS

This section outlines the history of Microsoft Windows and then takes an in-depth look at the differences among the many versions of Microsoft's flagship operating system. That way you can sort out the essentials for today's techs from the many varieties you'll hear about. Microsoft entered the operating system game in the early 1980s with a command line OS called Microsoft Disk Operating System, or MS-DOS. With a command-line OS, you interacted with the computer to run programs and save files and all the other computing functions by typing and then pressing the ENTER key on your keyboard. This whole typing thing worked for people who could memorize commands and such, but alternative operating systems, such as the Apple Macintosh, offered a visual interface, where you could interact with the computer by clicking on pictures. The time came for Microsoft to step up its game and produce a graphical user interface (GUI) where users could use a mouse to point and click.

Early Windows

The earliest version of Windows, Microsoft Windows 1.0, dates from 1985 and was little more than a graphical overlay of the DOS command-line operating system. This overlay version of Windows went through a number of updates, ending with the first truly popular version of Windows, Windows for Workgroups version 3.1 (Figure 3.2).

Figure 3.2: Windows for Workgroups

Note

Microsoft released several versions of Windows 3.1, with minor differences in name. Techs call the versions collectively Windows 3.x. In 1989, Microsoft offered a completely separate version of Windows called Windows NT. Windows NT was a true graphical operating system and was dramatically more powerful then the Windows overlay versions. Windows NT also cost more than other versions of Windows, however, and saw little adoption outside of servers and systems where users needed a lot of power. Windows NT went through a number of versions, culminating with Windows NT 4.0 in 1996 (Figure 3.3).

Comparing Windows NT to the old overlay versions of Windows is akin to comparing the first computer game you ever played to the games we play today: technically the same thing (a game), but that's about it. Windows NT had so many features that showing them all could take days, but one is important. NT came with a new way to organize hard drives and files, called the NT File System (NTFS). Before NTFS, all versions of Windows used an ancient file system called the file allocation table (FAT).

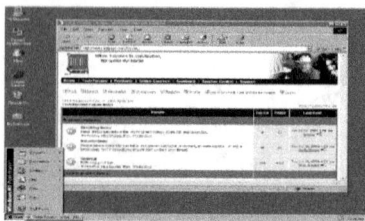

Figure 3.3: Windows NT 4.0

FAT was great when first invented in the late 1970s, but by the mid-80s it was showing its age. NTFS took care of a number of problems, the biggest of which was security. FAT had no security. There was no way to control what people did with your files. NTFS was built from the ground up with security in mind. We'll cover both FAT and NTFS later in the book, but for now appreciate that only Windows NT had NTFS. It wasn't until 1995 that Microsoft dumped the overlay concept and introduced Windows 95, the first version of Windows for the standard user that was also a full-blown operating system (Figure 3.4). Windows 95 offered many improvements over Windows 3.x, and eventually Microsoft released several upgraded versions as well, such as: Windows 95, Windows 98 SE, and Windows Me. The upgraded versions continued to use the FAT file system. Over the years, Windows has gone through massive changes and a large number of improved versions. The later versions have nothing in common with earlier versions other than the name "Windows."

NOTE: When we describe Windows 95, 98, 98 SE, and Me from a historical Stand point, we lump them all together, using the term "Windows 9x."

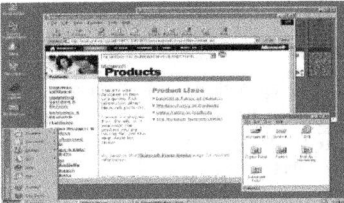

Figure 3.4: Windows 95

Modern Windows

The vast majority of computers in the field today run one of the three modern families of Windows, we focuses on those as well: Windows 2000, Windows XP, and Windows Vista. But as you know from Table 3.1 at the beginning of this chapter, just saying the name of a Windows family doesn't do the varieties within that family justice. The trick is to organize these versions in such a way to discover their similarities and differences. In this section, we'll look at versions of Windows 2000, XP, and Vista, as well as a few other versions of Windows, and see the differences in detail.

A great place to start is with the arrival of Windows 2000 in 2001. Throughout most of the 1990s, before Windows 2000 came along (followed very quickly by Windows XP), Windows was in a bit of a mess. Microsoft had two totally different operating systems? each called Windows ?that it sold for two different markets. Microsoft sold the Windows 9x series for the home user and small office, and the much more powerful Windows NT series for corporate environments.

3.4   ESSENTIALS OF WINDOWS 2000

Windows 2000 was the first step toward changing this mess. It was based on the old Windows NT (including support for NTFS), but for the first time it included a great interface, provided support for dang near any program, and was substantially easier to use than the old Windows NT. Microsoft originally presented Windows 2000 as a replacement for Windows NT, but its stability and ease of use motivated many knowledgeable Windows 9x users to upgrade to Windows 2000. Windows 2000 started to appear as "the single Windows to replace all the other versions." Windows 2000 came in two versions: Professional and Server.

But a good tech should at least know that these server versions exist. If you were to look at the Windows 2000 Server desktop, you'd be hard pressed to see any obvious differences from the Windows 2000 Professional version. Don't let Windows 2000 Server fool you (Figure 3.5). Windows Server is a heavy-duty version, loaded with extra software and features that make it superb for running an office server. Windows Server versions are also extremely expensive, costing on average of around $200 per computer that accesses the server.

Windows XP

Windows XP came hot on the heels of Windows 2000. Under the hood, XP was basically the same as Windows 2000, but added a dramatically improved interface and a number of new features, such as a built-in CD writer. Microsoft also broke with the beauty of 2000's "one OS for everyone" idea. Microsoft visualized three types of users professionals, home users, and media junkiesso Windows XP came in several versions, such as Windows XP Professional, Windows XP Home, and Windows XP Media Centre.

Windows XP Professional

Microsoft Windows XP Professional is, in many people's opinions, the most versatile and, therefore, the most mainstream version of Windows XP. Microsoft tuned Windows XP Professional for office environments with many users sharing lots of data and multiple users sharing single computers. Windows XP Professional provides full-blown data security, and it is the only version of Windows XP with the capability of logging into a special Windows Server-controlled network called a *domain*.

A Windows domain is a group of networked computers all under the control of a single computer running some version of Windows Server. Users on a domain can make a single login to their computer that defines everything they can do on every other computer on the domain.

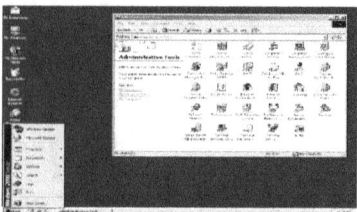

Figure 3.5: Windows 2000 Server

Windows XP Home

As its name implies, Windows XP Home is designed for the home and small-office user. Windows XP Home is a stripped-down version of XP Professional. The best way to describe Windows XP Home is to list the Windows XP Professional features that Windows XP Home lacks. Windows XP Home does *not* have

♦　**The ability to log on to a Windows domain** A Windows Home PC may log into any single Windows server, but you must have a user name and password on every single server. With a domain, you can have one user name and password that works on all computers that are members of the domain.

♦　**Encrypting file system** With Windows XP Professional, you can encrypt a file or a folder so that only you can read it. Windows XP Home edition lacks this feature.

♦　**Support for multiple processors** Windows XP Home does not support more than one physical CPU. Windows XP Professional supports two separate CPUs.

Note CPU support is based on physical CPUs, not the number of cores in a single CPU. See Chapter 2, "Microprocessors," for details on multi-core CPUs.

Figure 3.6 Windows XP Professional

♦   **Support for Remote Desktop:** A Windows XP Professional PC may be remotely accessed from another computer by using the Remote Desktop (Figure 3.7). You cannot access a Windows XP Home system in this fashion.

♦   **Support for NTFS Access Control:** The NTFS file system is capable of powerful controls on what users may do to a file or folder. Windows XP Home doesn't give you the ability to control these NTFS permissions individually. When you look at the properties of a file or folder in Windows XP Home, you'll notice that there is no Security tab. Instead, Windows XP Home's sharing tab (Figure 3.8) shows that only one folder, the Shared Documents folder, is open for sharing? Very different from XP Professional.

♦   **Support for Group Policies** Do you need to keep users from using a certain program? Do you want to prevent them from changing the screensaver? What do you want to do if they try to log in three times unsuccessfully? That's the job of group polices. Well, if you want this level of control on your system, get Windows XP Professional, because XP Home doesn't support them.

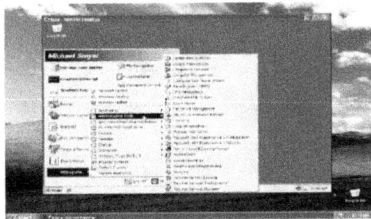

Figure 3.7:   Remote Desktop

A few more differences exist between Windows XP Professional and XP Home, but these are the ones you're most likely to run into. Basically, if you want serious control of the folders, files, users, and network, you need XP Professional.

Windows XP Media Centre

Microsoft Media Centre is a specialized XP version that includes the very handy Windows Media Centre program (Figure 3.8). Media Centre is a Personal Video Recorder (PVR) program that enables you to watch and record television (you'll need a TV tuner card) and organize all of your media, from photos to music.

On the Microsoft Media Centre Web site, Microsoft declares that the Windows XP Microsoft Media Centre edition is based on Windows XP Professional; however, other than the Media Centre program, Windows XP Media Centre's capabilities are identical to those of Windows XP Home.

Windows Vista

Even though Windows 7 is available, Windows Vista is the latest version of Windows on the current CompTIA A+ exams. It's important to recognize Vista and know what choices you have when deciding which version of Vista you need for a particular PC. Windows has a number of versions of Vista, each geared toward a particular market segment. Let's look at the most common versions of Vista.

Windows Vista Home Basic

Windows Vista Home Basic is roughly equivalent to Windows XP Home. Microsoft gears it to home users not needing more advanced multimedia support.

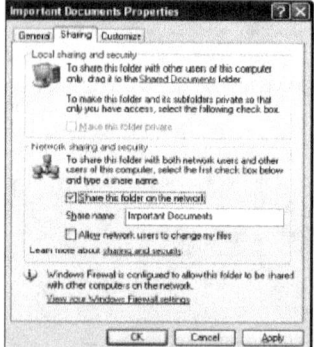

Figure 3.8: Windows XP Home Sharing Tab

Windows Vista Home Premium

Windows Vista Home Premium (Figure 3.10) is the same as Windows Vista Home Basic, but it adds an upgraded Windows Media Centre PVR application, similar to the one found in Windows XP Media Centre.

Windows Vista Business

Windows Vista Business is the basic business version and has all the security, file sharing, and access controls seen in Windows XP Professional.

Windows Vista Ultimate

Windows Vista Ultimate combines all of the features of every other Vista version and includes some other features, such as a game performance tweaker and DVD ripping capability (Figure 3.11).

Figure 3.9: Microsoft Media Centre

Figure 3.10: Vista Home Premium Media Centre

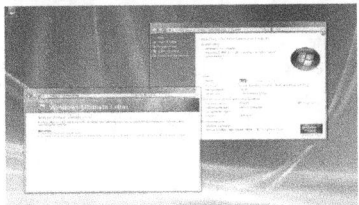

Figure 3.11: Vista Ultimate

Enter 64-bit Windows

From roughly 1986 to around 2001, all CPUs were 32-bit. While we will save the big discussion of what 32-bit means for "Microprocessors," for now let's keep it simple: a 32-bit CPU can only use a maximum of 4 gigabytes of RAM ($232 = 4,294,967,296$). Starting in 2001 we began to see 64-bit CPUs that could accept more than 4 gigabytes. 64-bit CPUs are now extremely common.

Note CPUs and 32- and 64-bit processing are covered in much greater detail in Chapter 2, "Microprocessors." The leap from 32-bit to 64-bit processing has a number of advantages. The really big compelling reason to go from 32- to 64-bit is that 64-bit CPUs support more than 4 gigabytes of RAM. The more RAM you have, the more programsand the bigger the programsyour system will run. Until fairly recently, not too many of us cared to go above 4 gigabytes of RAM. We didn't need the RAM and we didn't have a CPU that could run at 64-bits. My, how things have changed over the past few years!

Remember that 32-bit CPUs can support up to 4 GB of RAM. In concept, 64-bit CPUs can support up to 16 *terabytes* of memory, although you certainly won't find that much memory in the typical

PC. The 64-bit CPUs first showed up with the Intel Itanium back in 2001. At that time the only folks interested in 64-bit processing were large data centres and a few organizations that needed to crunch big numbers. To run a computer with an Itanium, you needed an operating system that worked with a 64-bit processor. Up to this point, every version of Windows only ran at 32-bit. Microsoft answered the call by creating special 64-bit versions of Windows 2000 and XP, but these 64-bit versions of Windows 2000 were very rare.

In 2003, Advanced Micro Devices (AMD) started to ship the popular Athlon 64- bit CPU. This CPU could run in either 32-bit or 64-bit mode, making 64-bit a realistic option for most of us. Intel followed AMD around 2004 with Pentium 4 CPUs also capable of 32-bit or 64-bit processing. Since then, almost every CPU sold by Intel or AMD has the ability to run in either 32-bit or 64-bit mode. Moving from the 32-bit to the 64-bit world is easy, but only if you have a version of Windows to support 64-bit. Microsoft has multiple versions of Windows designed to support 64-bit CPUs.

Note All 32-bit versions of Windows support a maximum of 4 gigabytes of RAM. If your PC has more than 4 gigabytes and you're not running 64-bit Windows, you might as well remove any RAM above 4 gigabytes. You're wasting it!

Windows XP 64-bit Versions
The 64-bit-only version of Windows XP was called Windows XP 64-bit Edition (apparently Microsoft decided not to get cute when naming that one). Given that it only worked on Intel Itanium processors, the chance of your seeing this operating system is pretty small unless you decide to work in a place with powerful server needs. The Windows XP Professional x64 Edition is much more common, as it runs on any AMD or Intel processor that supports both 32 and 64 bits (Figure 3.12).

Figure 3.12: Windows XP Professional x64 Edition

Windows XP 64-bit versions have had some impact, as they were the first stable Windows versions that truly supported 64-bit processing, but it was the introduction of Microsoft Vista that really started the move into the 64-bit world.

Windows Vista 64-bit Versions
Every one of the earlier listed Vista versions comes in both a 32-bit and 64-bit versions. As we move into PCs with more than 4 gigabytes of RAM, it's important to make sure your version of Windows is a 64-bit version (Figure 3.13).

Note : Every version of Windows 7 comes in 32-bit and 64-bit on the same install disc.

3.5   TRANSITIONING TO 64-BIT WINDOWS

Techs use the x# terminology to describe particular computer architecture, implying that there is some compatibility within that architecture. This matters because people need some comfort that the software they purchase will work properly with the computer they have. The transition from 32-bit versions of Windows to 64-bit versions of Windows requires a certain update in terminology.

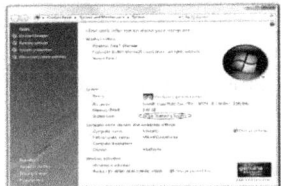

Figure 3.13: 64-bit Vista

x86 versus x64 Intel originally used numbers to name its CPUs, such as 8086, 80286, 80386, and so on. To talk about them collectively, the industry replaced the leading numbers with an x and kept the numbers that stayed consistent for all the processors, thus x86 describes the Intel CPU architecture for PCs. All the 32-bit versions of Windows were designed to run on x86 architecture.

The move to 64-bit CPUs and, equally importantly, to 64-bit versions of Windows required some sort of change in terminology. Microsoft and others picked up the x# terminology and changed it to market 64-bit-only versions of their software, branding the 64-bit software as *x64*. A consumer, therefore, could look at a product such as Windows XP Professional x64 Edition and very quickly know that the software was designed for 64-bit CPUs rather than 32-bit CPUs. The two x# uses x86 and x64 don't really compare, but that's okay. Computer people love the letter *X* almost as much as car manufacturers do.

Software Compatibility: Transitions to updated architecture, such as the change from x86 to x64, creates concern among users, because they fear that their old programs won't run or will run poorly, or that they'll have problems with compatibility down the road. Techs need to allay those fears by educating users properly. Here's the scoop in a nutshell. Most of the 64-bit processors run either 32-bit or 64-bit versions of Windows without missing a beat. The 64-bit versions of Windows require a 64-bit CPU; they snicker at 32-bit (or x86) processors and refuse to play. Many companies have produced 64-bit versions of application software that only works with 64-bit Windows running with a 64-bit CPU. Great, right? But what about all those 32-bit applications out there working for a living? It gets interesting.

Windows Vista 64-bit versions support most 32-bit applications, sometimes without any user intervention and sometimes through explicit use of the Windows compatibility mode options. (Just for the record, you sometimes need to use Windows compatibility mode options to run older programs on Windows Vista 32-bit versions, so it's not just a function of 64-bit support for 32-bit apps.) Windows can try to emulate previous versions of Windows if an application balks at loading. To run a program in an emulated version of Windows, you need to access the primary executable file that, when double-clicked, makes the program run. We'll go through where to find your program files in the various versions of Windows later in this chapter, but a quick example should suffice here. A user has a custom programcalled "Widgets for XP"designed to take advantage of particular features in Windows XP Professional with Service Pack 2 installed and it doesn't work in Windows Vista. Open Computer and go to C:\Program Files\Widgets for XP and look for a file with the type listed as Application, such as WidgetsXP.exe (Figure 3.14). Right-click and select Properties. On the Compatibility tab, you can select the checkbox next to *Run this program in compatibility mode for*: and select the OS of choice (Figure 3.15). In this case, we would select Windows XP (Service Pack 2) to provide optimal compatibility for the application.

Windows saves the configuration change and tries to open the program in compatibility mode each time the program loads.

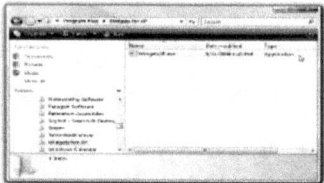

Figure 3.14: Finding an Executable File

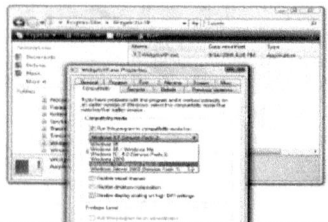

Figure 3.15: Compatibility Mode Options

The Windows Interface

All versions of Windows share certain characteristics, configuration files, and general look and feel. Here's some good news: You'll find the same, or nearly the same, utilities in almost all versions of Windows, and once you master one versionboth GUI and command-line interfaceyou'll pretty much have them all covered. This section covers the essentials: where to find things, how to makeover, and what common utilities are available. Where versions of Windows differ in concept or detail, I'll point that out along the way. You'll get to the underlying structure of Windows in the subsequent two sections of this chapter. For now, let's look at the common user interface.

User Interface

Windows offers a set of utilities, or *interfaces*, that every user should know aboutboth how and why to access them.

Login

Logging into a Windows computer is something we all do, but few of us take time to appreciate. Your user name and password define what you can do on your computer. Every version of Windows supports multiple users on a single machine, so the starting point for any tour of the Windows user interface starts with the *login screen.* Figure 4.16 shows the old, ugly, but very functional Windows 2000 login screen.

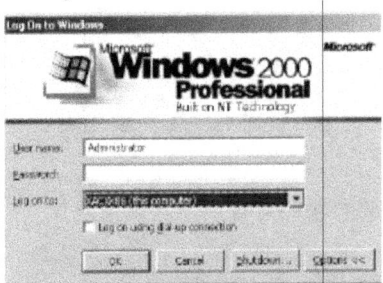

Figure 3.16: Windows 2000 login screen

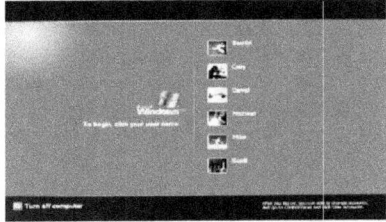

Figure 3.17: Windows XP Welcome Screen

Microsoft improved the login screen in XP, creating a new type of login called the *Welcome screen* (Figure 3.17). If you're using Windows XP Home or Media Centre, this is the only login screen you will see. Windows XP Professional also has the Welcome screen. If you're running a Windows XP Professional system that connects to a Windows domain, however, you go right back to the classic login screen (Figure 3.18).

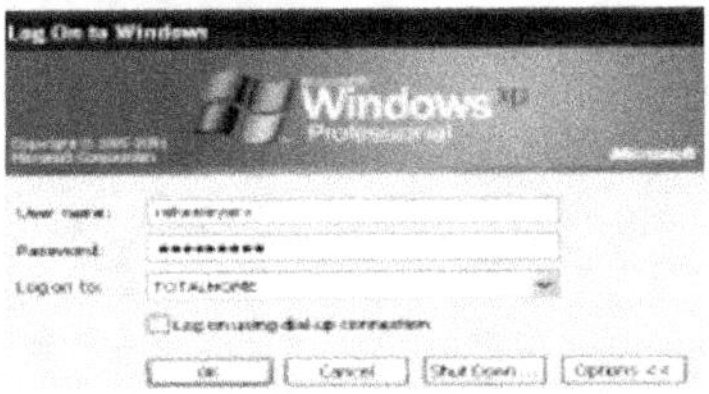

Figure 3.18: Windows XP domain login screen

Windows Vista dumped the old login screen entirely. All versions of Windows Vista use an improved version of XP's Welcome screen (Figure 3.19).

Figure 3.19: Windows Vista Welcome Screen
Desktop

The Windows *desktop* is your primary interface to the computer. The desktop is always there, underneath whatever applications you have opened. The desktop analogy appeals to most people we're used to sitting down at a desk to get work done. Figure 3.20 shows a nice, clean Windows XP desktop; note the icons on the left and the various graphical elements across the bottom. You can add folders and files to the desktop and customize the background to change its colour or add a picture. Most people like to do so certainly, I do! As an example, Figure 3.21 shows the desktop from my home system a Windows Vista Ultimate PC.

Note Your desktop is actually a folder in your computer. Whatever is in that folder shows up on your desktop. It's critical that you know how to get to that folder in every version of Windows covered on. Read on.

Clearly the Vista desktop differs a lot compared to the Windows XP desktop. What you're seeing is something called the Aero desktop. *Aero* desktop adds a number of impressive aesthetic features to your desktop that Microsoft claims makes the user experience more enjoyable and productive. I'm not going to get into an argument on the value of the Aero desktop, but it is an important part of the Windows Vista and Windows 7 interface.

Figure 3.20: Windows XP Desktop

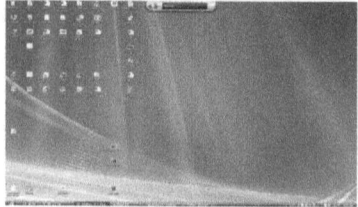

Figure 3.21: Mike's Messy Desktop

Figure 3.22: Transparency

Flip 3D enables you to view and select all of your open Windows in a 3-D format as shown in Figure 3.23. It's actually very handy once you start using it.

Figure 3.23. Flip 3D

Flip 3D is fun to use. Press the WINDOWS KEY-TAB key combination to start it. Keep pressing the key combination to cycle through the windows. When the window you want is in the forefront, release the keys, and that window will be the active window on your screen. Try WINDOWS KEY-TAB-SHIFT to scroll through your windows in the opposite direction.

To use the Aero desktop, you must have a video card that supports Aero. "Video," but for now here's what Microsoft says your video needs:

- DirectX 9 capability or better
- At least 128 megabytes of video RAM
- Windows Display Driver Model (WDDM) driver
- Pixel Shader version 2.0

When you install Vista, the installer checks your video to determine if it can support Aero. If your video card is capable, Aero is turned on automatically.

On an installed system, press the WINDOWS KEY-TAB combination. If the Flip 3D appears, you have Aero. If it doesn't, Aero is not active. To turn on Aero, right-click on your desktop and then select the Personalize menu option. Next, select Window Colour and Appearance. If you see a screen that looks like Figure 3.24, you already have Aero running. Select the Windows Aero colour scheme to activate the Aero desktop.

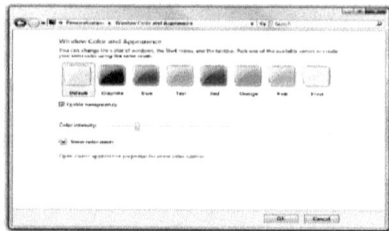

Figure 3.24: You've got Aero!

Note If you can't run on Aero desktop, you need to upgrade your system to meet the minimum requirements. This usually means a new video card or updated video card drivers. If you're running Aero, note that the Window Colour and Appearance screen shown in Figure 3.24 has a slider to adjust the transparency settings and a checkbox to turn transparency off completely. The WINDOWS KEY-T combination gives a preview of all minimized windows. ALT-TAB gives a preview of all running windows. Try Aero. It may not be the productivity tool Microsoft promises it to be, but it sure is fun.

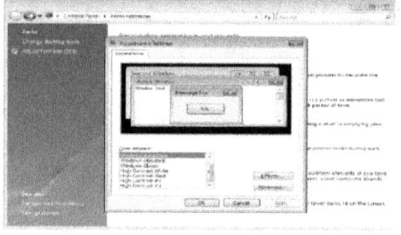

Figure 3.25: The lack of transparency and the flat window with no drop shadow shows that Aero is not activated.

Taskbar and Start Menu

The *taskbar* runs along the bottom of all Windows desktops and includes up to four sections (depending on the version of Windows and your configuration). Starting at the left side, these are the Start button, the Quick Launch toolbar, the running programs area, and the notification area. Although the taskbar by default sits at the bottom of the desktop, you can move it to either side or to the top of the screen. One of the main jobs of the taskbar is to show the *Start button*, probably the most licked button on all Windows systems. You can find the Start button on the far left end of the taskbar. Figure 3.26 shows the Start buttons for Windows 2000, Windows XP, and Windows Vista (in order). Click the Start button to bring up the Start menu, where you can see the applications installed on the system and start them. Now,

Figure 3.26: Windows 2000 XP

Three different Windows Start buttons move your mouse cursor onto the All Programs (Windows XP) or Programs (all other versions) menu item. When the All Programs/Programs menu appears, move the cursor to the Accessories menu. Locate the Notepad program and click it. By default, Windows hides lesser-used menu options, so if you don't see Notepad, click the double down arrows at the bottom of the Accessories menu to make Notepad appear.

Note You have a lot of clicking to do in this chapter, so take a moment to reflect on what I call the General Rules of Clicking. With a few exceptions, these rules always apply, and they really help in manipulating the Windows interface to do whatever you need done:

♦   Click menu items once to use them.

♦   Click icons once to select them.

♦   Click icons twice to use them.

♦   Right-click anything and select Properties to see its properties.

Great! If you opened Notepad properly, you should see something like Figure, with Notepad displaying an untitled text page. Notice how Notepad shows up on the taskbar at the bottom of your screen. Most running programs appear on the taskbar in this way. Close the Notepad program by clicking on the button with the X in the upper right corner of the Notepad window. Look again at the taskbar to see that Notepad no longer appears there.

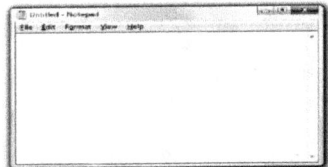

Figure 3.27: Notepad application (note the buttons in the upper-right corner)

Now look all the way to the right end of the taskbar. This part of the taskbar is known officially as the *notification area*, though many techs and the CompTIA A+ certification exams call it the *system tray*. You will at a minimum see the current time displayed in the system tray, and on most Windows systems you'll also see a number of small icons there Now look all the way to the right end of the taskbar.

Figure 3.28 shows the system tray on my PC.

Figure 3.28: System tray showing several icons and the time

Most programs run in a window. Background programs function like any other program except they do not use a window, simply because the nature of their particular jobs makes a window unnecessary thousands of programs like to run in the system tray: network status, volume controls battery state (on laptops), and removable device status are just a few examples. What shows up on yours depends on your version of Windows, what hardware you use, and what background programs you have installed. Some of the icons in Figure 3.28, for example, include my antivirus program, a handy notification program for incoming Facebook and Twitter messages, and my UPS program.

Near the left end of the taskbar, next to the Start button, you will find the *Quick Launch toolbar* (**Figure 3.29**), a handy extra where you can select often-used programs with a single click. On Windows XP systems, the Quick Launch toolbar is not displayed on the taskbar by default, so before you can use this convenient feature, you must right-click the taskbar, select Properties, and check Show Quick Launch. To change the contents of the Quick Launch toolbar, simply drag icons onto or off of it.

Figure 3.29: Quick Launch Toolbar

The Many Faces of Windows Explorer

Windows Explorer enables you to manipulate files and folders stored on all the drives in or connected to your computer. Microsoft presents the tool in a variety of ways to help you focus quickly on what you want to accomplish. If you want to see the contents of an optical disc, for example, you can open *My Computer* (Windows 2000/XP) or *Computer* (Windows Vista/7) by double-clicking the icon on the desktop or selecting the icon from the Start menu to have Windows Explorer open with the drives displayed (Figure 3.30). To display the contents of a drive or folder, double-click it.

Windows Explorer in Windows 2000 has a fairly Spartan interface, whereas Windows XP offers a series of common tasks in a bar along the left side of the screen, as you can see in Figure 3-30. Windows Vista also offers tasks, but the options display in a bar below the location bar, near the top of the window (Figure 3.31).

When you access My Documents (Windows 2000/XP) or Documents (Windows Vista/7) by double-clicking the icon on the desktop or selecting from the Start menu, Windows opens Windows Explorer with your user folders displayed. Because your My Documents/Documents folder is stored (by default) on the C: hard drive, Windows Explorer shows the contents of that drive, drilled down specifically to your folders.

The fact that one way to open Windows Explorer is to double-click My Computer or Computer, and another way to open Windows Explorer is to double-click My Documents or Documentsand the two methods show different contents initiallyleads many users to assume that they have two distinct tools. That's simply not the case.

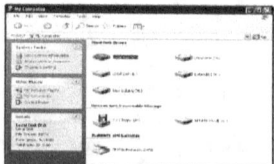

Figure 3.30: Windows Explorer in Windows XP displaying the drives installed, as well as common tasks on the left.

Windows Explorer changes what's displayed to suit specific tasks preset by Microsoft, but it's a single tool that can point to different locations on your computer. Even better, you can change the look of Windows Explorer by clicking a button. The Folders button in Windows 2000 and Windows XP toggles the *Folders list* on or off on the left (Figure 3.32). The Folders list is a tree menu that enables you to move the focus of Windows Explorer to different folders or drives. The Folders list replaces the common tasks bar in Windows XP. Note that the Folders list is enabled by default in Windows Vista no matter whether you open the tool through Computer or Documents.

In Windows Vista, you can alter the view of Windows Explorer in several ways. On the task bar, you can click the down arrow next to Views to change the size of the icons, the details displayed, and more. You can turn off the Folders list if desired by clicking the down arrow next to Organize and then selecting Layout from the menu options.

The Folders list view makes copying and moving files and folders from one location to another very easy. The steps differ slightly when you copy to a folder on the same drive versus when you copy to a folder on a different drive, although the first step is the same: Select a folder in the Folders list, and the contents of that folder appear in the main pane on the right.

Figure 3.31: Windows Explorer in Windows Vista displaying the drives installed and showing tasks

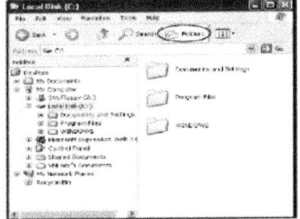

Figure 3.32: Windows Explorer in Windows XP with the Folders list toggled on

To move or copy a file from one folder to another folder on the same drive, click and hold a file or folder in the main pane and then drag the cursor over to any folder in the Folders list. A ? symbol will appear in Windows Vista and 7, although not in Windows 2000 or XP. Release the mouse button, and you move that file or folder to the new folder. If you want to copy a file or folder rather than move it, press the CTRL key on your keyboard and then click and drag into the desired folder. The ? symbol (if any) changes to a +; release the mouse button to copy the file or folder.

To copy or move a file from one folder to another folder on a different drive, click and hold a file or folder in the main pane and then drag the cursor over to any folder in the Folders list, and a + symbol will appear. Release the mouse button, and you'll make a copy of that file or folder in the new folder. If you want to move a file or folder rather than just copy it, press the SHIFT key on your keyboard and then click and drag into the desired folder. The + symbol changes to a ? in Windows Vista/7 or just goes away in Windows 2000/XP; release the mouse button to move the file or folder.

Notice the differences in the icons displayed in Windows Explorer? Windows assigns different icons to different types of files, based on their *extensions*, the set of characters at the end of a filename, such as .EXE, .TXT, or .JPG. The oldest extensions, starting from back in the DOS era, are usually three characters, but current programs may use two-character extensions, such as .JS (JavaScript) or .AU (audio), or even four-character extensions, such as the ubiquitous .HTML for Web pages. In rare cases, a filename might actually have no extension.

As you look at these icons on your own screen, some of you might say, "But I don't see any extensions!" That's because Windows hides them by default. To see the extensions in 2000/XP, select Tools | Folder Options to open the Folder Options dialog box (Figure 3.33). Click the View tab and uncheck *Hide extensions for known file types*. In Vista, click on Organize | Folder and Search Options | View tab to see the same dialog box.

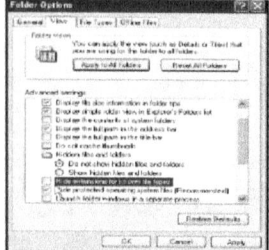

Figure 3.33: Folder Options dialog box

There are two other very handy settings under the View tab, but to see the results well, you need to be in the C: drive of My Computer, as shown in Figure 3.34.

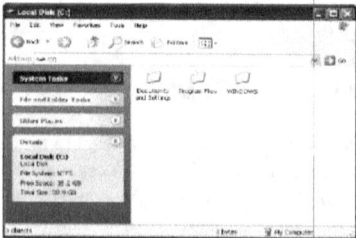

Figure 3.34: Default My Computer view where many things are hidden

Go back into the View tab under Folder Options, click the *Show hidden files and folder s*radio button, and then uncheck *Hide protected operating system files*. Click the *Apply to folders* button in Windows Vista, the *Apply to all folders* button in Windows XP, or the Apply button in Windows 2000. Your C: drive should look like Figure 3.35 it shows.

Figure 3.35 My Computer displaying hidden files and folders Go back into the View tab under Folder Options, click the *Show hidden files and folders* radio button, and then uncheck *Hide protected operating system files*. Click the *Apply to folders* button in Windows Vista, the *Apply to all folders* button in Windows XP, or the Apply button in Windows 2000. Your C: drive should look like Figure 3.35 (it shows the Windows XP version) when you are finished. As before, when you return to examining the folder contents, you will see the file extensions, and possibly some previously hidden files.

Now that those files are visible, you have the awesome responsibility of keeping them safe. In general, the less you handle your vital system files, the better. You'll learn some ways to do useful things with files that were previously hidden, but unless you really know what you're doing, it's best to leave them alone. Before you turn a PC over to someone who isn't a trained PC tech, you'll probably want to hide those system files again. Microsoft has tried to help users organize their files and folders through various user folders and subfolders that you access through Windows Explorer. The different operating systems offer different choices, so let's look at My Documents and the User's Files.

My Documents, My [Whatever] All versions of Windows provide a special folder structure for each user account so users have their own places to store personal data. This folder grouping is called *My Documents* in Windows 2000 and XP. Many Windows programs take advantage of My Documents and by default store their files in the folder or in a subfolder.

Windows XP installations do not show My Documents on the desktop by default. On Windows XP, you can access it readily through the Start menu, or you can add it to your desktop. Right-click the desktop and select Properties to open the Display Properties dialog box. Select the Desktop tab, and then click on the Customize Desktop button to open the Desktop Items dialog box (Figure 3.36). On the General tab, select the checkbox next to My Documents, My Computer, or both, and then click OK to close the dialog box and make any selected icons appear on the desktop.

Figure 3.36: XP Desktop Items dialog box

Note As with most tools in Windows, Microsoft gives you more than one way to accomplish tasks. In XP and Vista, try right-clicking the Start menu icon, selecting Properties, and choosing the Classic Start Menu radio button

Figure 3.37: My Pictures Subfolder in My Documents

Windows XP adds a number of subfolders to My Documents: My Pictures (which offers filmstrip and thumbnail views of pictures you store there), My Music (which will fire up Media Player to play any file), My Videos (which, again, starts Media Player), and more. Figure 3.37 shows My Pictures, using the thumbnail view.

User's Files Windows Vista takes the equivalent of My Documents to a whole new level with the *User's Files* option. (Although a Documents folder is available, it's designed literally for documents, such as text files.) Click on the Start menu and you'll see a folder option with the user name of the account that's currently logged into the computer. With that option, not only do you get all of the folders you get in Windows 2000/XP, but Vista also adds a number of other folders as well as interesting but important data such as your Internet Explorer favourites and copies of recent searches.

Just as with Windows XP, the user's folder does not show on the desktop by default. To see this folder, right-click on the desktop, select Personalize, and then click *Change desktop icons* on the left of the Personalization window. You'll see a Desktop Icon Setting dialog box where you can select the User's File option to display the personal files of the logged-in user account. Figure 3.38 shows the User's Files folder for my editor, with the Desktop Icon Settings dialog box in the background. No matter what your version of Windows decides to call it, My Documents/User's Files is an incredibly critical part of your computer's directory structure. Not only does this store your most personal (and important) documents, it also stores most of the personalization settings for each user. You'll see more of My Documents/User's Files in the next section.

Figure 3.38 Typical user accounts folder in Windows Vista

Recycle Bin

In Windows, a file is not erased when you delete it. Windows adds a level of protection in the form of a special folder called the *Recycle Bin*. When you delete a file in Windows, the file moves into the Recycle Bin. It stays there until you empty the Recycle Bin or restore the file, or until the Recycle Bin reaches a preset size and starts erasing its oldest contents.

To access the Recycle Bin's properties, right-click the icon and select Properties. The Recycle Bin's properties look different in different versions of Windows, but they all work basically the same. Figure 3.39 shows the properties of a typical Windows XP Recycle Bin. Note that you set the amount of drive space to use for the Recycle Bin, 10 percent being the default amount. If a hard drive starts to run low on space, this is one of the first places to check.

Figure 3.39: Windows XP Recycle Bin Properties

My Network Places/Network

Systems tied to a network, either via a network cable or by a modem, have a folder called *My Network Places* in XP or simply *Network* in Vista (see Figure 3.40). This shows all the current network connections available to you. You'll learn about My Network Places and "Local Area Networking" in the subsequent chapters.

Windows Sidebar

Windows Vista comes with a UI feature called the *Windows Sidebar*, a tool that sits on the desktop and enables small helper applications called Microsoft Gadgets to run. You can display a clock, for example, or a dynamic weather update.

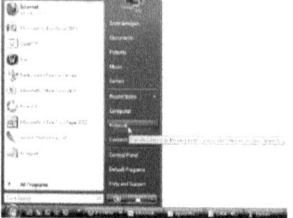

Figure 3.40 Network in Windows Vista

Windows XP

Recycle Bin Properties handful of Gadgets, but developers have gone crazy with them, enabling you to add all sorts of useful tools, such as the Twitter feed and World of Warcraft search and realm status Gadgets in Figure 3.41.

Hot Keys

In Windows, you can use key combinations to go directly to various programs and places. Here's a fairly extensive list of general-purpose commands for Windows. Be aware that some applications may change the use of these commands.

Function Keys

♦ **F1** Help
♦ **F2** Rename
♦ **F3** Search menu
♦ **F5** Refresh the current window
♦ **F6** Move among selections in current windows

Figure 3.41: Windows Sidebar in action

Popular Hot Keys

♦   **CTRL-ESC** Open Start menu

♦   **ALT-TAB** Switch between open programs

♦   **ALT-F4** Quit program

♦   **CTRL-Z** Undo the last command

♦   **CTRL-A** Select all the items in the current window

♦   **SHIFT-DELETE** Delete item permanently

♦   **SHIFT-F10** Open a shortcut menu for the selected item (this is the same as right clicking an object)

♦   **SHIFT** Bypass the automatic-run feature for optical media (by pressing and holding down the SHIFT key while you insert optical media)

♦   **ALT-SPACE** Display the main window's System menu (from this menu you can restore, move, resize, minimize, maximize, or close the window)

♦   **ALT-ENTER** Open the properties for the selected object

Working with Text

♦   **CTRL-C** Copy

♦   **CTRL-X** Cut

♦   **CTRL-V** Paste

♦   **CTRL-Z** Undo

Windows Key Shortcuts

These shortcuts use the special Windows key:

♦   **WINDOWS KEY** Start menu

♦   **WINDOWS KEY-D** Show desktop

♦   **WINDOWS KEY-E** Windows Explorer

♦   **WINDOWS KEY-L** Locks the computer

♦   **WINDOWS KEY-TAB** Cycle through taskbar buttons (or Flip 3D with Windows Aero in Vista)

♦   **WINDOWS KEY-BREAK** Open the System Properties dialog box

Operating System Folders

The modern versions of Windows organize essential files and folders in a relatively similar fashion. All have a primary system folder for storing most Windows internal tools and files. All have a set of folders for programs and user files. All use a special grouping of files called the Registry to keep track of all the hardware loaded and the drivers that enable you to use that hardware. Finally, every version has a RAM cache file, enabling more robust access to programs and utilities. Yet once you start to get into details, you'll find some very large differences. It's very important for you to know in some detail the location and function of many common folders and their contents.

System Folder

System Root is the tech name given to the folder in which Windows has been installed. System Root by default is C:\WINNT in Windows 2000, while Windows XP and Vista's System Root defaults to C:\WINDOWS. Be warned, these are defaults but not always the case; during the installation process, you can change where Windows is installed.

It's handy to know about System Root. You'll find it cropping up in many other tech publications, and you can specify it when adjusting certain Windows settings to make sure they work under all circumstances. When used as part of a Windows configuration setting, add percent signs (%) to the beginning and end like so: %System Root%.If you don't know where Windows is installed on a particular system, here's a handy trick. Get to a command prompt, type **cd %systemroot%**, and press ENTER. The prompt changes to the directory in which the Windows OS files are stored. Slick! "Working with the Command-Line Interface," for details on how to use the command prompt in Windows.

Let's run through the subfolders you should recognize and define (these folders are in all versions of Windows):

♦   **%SystemRoot%\FONTS** All of the fonts installed in Windows live here.

♦   **%SystemRoot%\Offline Files** when you tell your Web browser to save Web pages for offline viewing, they are stored in this folder. This is another folder that Windows automatically deletes if it needs the space.

♦   **%SystemRoot%\SYSTEM32** this is the *real* Windows! All of the most critical programs that make Windows run are stored here.

♦   **%SystemRoot%\Temp** Anytime Windows or an application running on Windows needs to create temporary files, they are placed here. Windows deletes these files automatically as needed, so never place an important file in this folder.

Program and Personal Document Folders
Windows has a number of important folders that help organize your programs and documents. They sit in the root directory at the same level as the system folder, and of course they have variations in name depending on the version of Windows. We'll assume that your computer is using a C: drivea pretty safe assumption, although there actually is a way to install all of Windows on a second hard-drive partition.

C:\Program Files (All Versions)
By default, most programs install some or all of their essential files into a subfolder of the Program Files folder. If you installed a program, it should have its own folder in here. Individual companies decide how to label their subfolders. Installing Photoshop made by Adobe, for example, creates the Adobe subfolder and then an Adobe Photoshop subfolder within it. Installing Silver light from Microsoft, on the other hand, only creates a Microsoft Silver light folder with the program files within it. (Some programmers choose to create a folder at the root of the C: drive, bypassing Program Files all together, but that's becoming increasingly rare.)

C:\Program Files (x86)
The 64-bit versions of Windows Vista and Windows 7 create two directory structures for program files. The 64-bit applications go into the C:\Program Files folder. The 32- bit applications, in contrast, go into the C:\Program Files (x86) folder. The separation makes it easy to find the proper

version of whatever application you seek.

Personal Documents

As you might expect, given the differences among the desktop names for personal document locations outlined earlier in the chapter, the personal folders for Windows 2000/XP and Windows Vista differ in location and name. Windows 2000 and Windows XP place personal folders in the Documents and Settings folder, whereas Windows Vista uses the Users folder. From there, they differ even more.

C:\Documents and Settings (2000 and XP) All of the personal settings for each user are stored here. All users have their own subfolders in Documents and Settings. In each user folder, you'll find another level of folders with familiar names such as Desktop, My Documents, and Start Menu. These folders hold the actual contents of these items.

• **\Documents and Settings\Default User (hidden)** All of the default settings for a user. For example, if the user doesn't specify a screensaver to use, Windows refers to this folder's settings to determine what screensaver it should use if needed.

•**\Documents and Settings\All Users** you can make settings for anyone who uses the computer. This is especially handy for applications: some applications are installed so all users may use them and some might be restricted to certain users. This folder stores information for any setting or application that's defined for all users on the PC.

•**\Documents and Settings\Shared Documents (XP Only)** If you're using XP's Simple File Sharing, this is the only folder on the computer that's shared.

•**\Documents and Settings\<User Name>** This folder stores all settings defined for a particular user (Figure 3-42). Opening any user's folder reveals a number of even lower folders. Each of these store very specific information about the user.

•**\Documents and Settings\<User Name>\Desktop** This folder stores the files on the user's desktop. If you delete this folder, you delete all the files placed on the desktop.

•**\Documents and Settings\<User Name>\<User name's>Documents** This is the My Documents folder for another user on the computer.

•**\Documents and Settings\<User Name>\Application Data (hidden)** This folder stores information and settings used by various programs that the user has installed.

•**\Documents and Settings\<User Name>\Start Menu** This folder stores any customizations the user made to the Start menu.

Figure 3.42 Contents of a typical \Documents and Settings folder in XP

C:\Users (Vista) Vista dumps the old Documents and Settings for the Users folder. Functionally similar to Documents and Settings, there are a number of sub-folders here that you need to know. Let's repeat the process, locating the same functions in their new locations.

•**\Users\Default (hidden), \Users\All Users,** All of these folders retain the same functions as in 2000/XP.

NOTE Vista and 7 make a special hidden folder called "Default User" that points to the User folder to support older applications.

•**\Users\<user name>** The big change takes place under each of the \Users\<username> folders. This folder still stores all settings defined for a particular user; however, this folder in Vista/7 is much more detailed than in 2000/XP (Figure 3.43

•**\Users\<User Name>\Desktop** Same as 2000/XP.

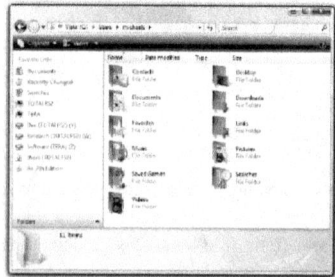

Figure 3.43 Contents of a typical \Users\<User Name>\folder in Vista

•**\Users\<User Name>\Documents** This is the Documents folder for that user. Compare the name of this folder to the one in Windows 2000/XP and know which is which.

•**\Users\<User Name>\Downloads** Microsoft's preferred download folder for applications to use. Most applications do use this folder, but some do not.

• **\Users\<User Name>\Start Menu** Same as 2000/XP.

EXAM TIP Be very careful here. Some of the folder name differences between 2000/XP and Vista/7 are subtle. Make sure you know the difference. Any good tech knows the name and function of all the folders just listed. As a tech, you will find yourself manually drilling into these folders for a number of reasons. Users rarely go directly into any of these folders with Windows Explorer. That's a good thing since, as a technician, you need to appreciate how dangerous it is for them to do so. Imagine a user going into a \Users\<User Name>\Desktop folder and wiping out someone's desktop folders. Luckily, Windows protects these folders by using NTFS permissions, making it very difficult for users to destroy anything other than their own work.

Registry

The *Registry* is a huge database that stores everything about your PC, including information on all of the hardware in the PC, network information, user preferences, file types, and virtually anything else you might run into with Windows. Almost any form of configuration you do to a Windows system involves editing the Registry. Every version of Windows stores the numerous Registry files (called *hives*) in the \%SystemRoot%\System32\config folder. Fortunately, you rarely have to access these massive files directly.

Windows Registry. You should, however, understand the basic components of the Registry, know how to edit the Registry manually, and know the best way to locate a particular setting.

Accessing the Registry

Before you look in the Registry, let's look at how you access the Registry directly by using a Registry editor. Once you know that, you can open the Registry on your machine and compare what you see to the examples in this chapter. Windows 2000 comes with two Registry editors: REGEDT32.EXE, shown in Figure 3.44, and the much older REGEDIT.EXE (Figure 3.45). You start either of these programs by going to a command prompt and typing its filename. The reason for having two different Registry editors is long and boring, and explaining it would require a very dull 15-minute monologue (preferably with an angelic chorus singing in the background) about how the Registry worked in Windows 9*x* and Windows NT. Suffice it to say that in Windows 2000, only REGEDT32 is safe to use for actual editing, but you can use the older REGEDIT to perform searches, because REGEDT32's search capabilities are not very good.

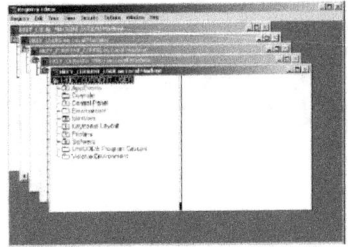

Figure 3.44 REGEDT32 in Windows 2000

Figure 3.45 REGEDIT in Windows 2000

Starting with Windows XP, Microsoft eliminated the entire two-Registry-editor nonsense by creating a new REGEDT32 that includes strong search functions. No longer are there two separate programs, but interestingly, entering either REGEDIT or REGEDT32 at a command prompt brings up the same program, so feel free to use either program name. We can also dispense with calling the Registry Editor by its filename and use its proper title.

Registry Components
The Registry is organized in a tree structure similar to the folders in the PC. Once you open the Registry Editor in Windows, you will see five main subgroups, or *root keys*:

♦   HKEY_CLASSES_ROOT
♦   HKEY_CURRENT_USER
♦   HKEY_USERS
♦   HKEY_LOCAL_MACHINE
♦   HKEY_CURRENT_CONFIG

Try opening one of these root keys by clicking on the plus sign to its left; note that more subkeys are listed underneath. A subkey also has other subkeys, or *values*. Figure 3.46 shows an example of a subkey with some values. Notice that the Registry Editor shows keys on the left and values on the right, just as Windows Explorer shows directories on the left and files on the right.

Note When writing about keys and values, I'll use the expression *key = value*.

Figure 4-46 Typical Registry keys and values

Figure 3.46 Typical Registry Keys and Values

The secret to understanding the Registry is to understand the function of the five root keys first. Each of these root keys has a specific function, so let's take a look at them individually.

HKEY_CLASSES_ROOT

This root key defines the standard *class objects* used by Windows. A class object is a named group of functions that define what you can do with the object it represents. Pretty much everything that has to do with files on the system is defined by a class object. For example, the Registry uses two class objects to define the popular MP3 sound file. If you search the Registry for the .MP3 file extension, you will find the first class object, which associates the .MP3 file extension with the name "Winamp.File" on this computer (Figure 3.47).

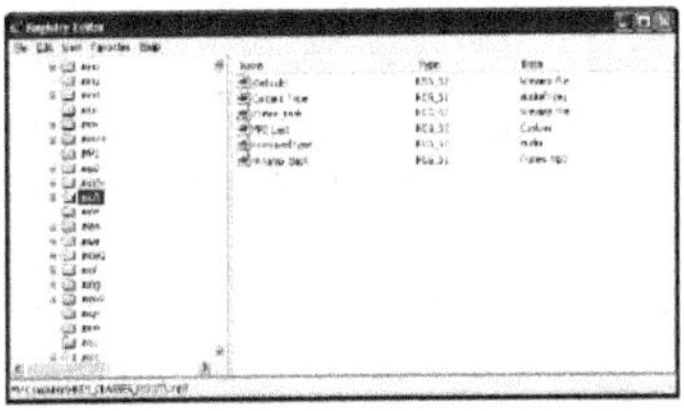

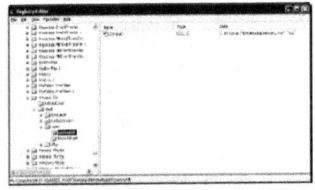

Figure 3.47 Association of .MP3 with Winamp

But what are the properties of Winamp.File? That's what the HKEY_CLASSES_ROOT root key is designed to handle. Search this section again for "Winamp.File" (or whatever it said is the value for your MP3 file) and look for a subkey called "open." This variable determines the *file association* (Figure 3.48), which is the Windows term for what program to use to open a particular type of file.

This subkey tells the system everything it needs to know about a particular software item, from which program to use to open a file, to the type of icon used to show the file, to what to show when you right-click on that file type. Although it is possible to change most of these settings in the Registry Editor, the normal way is to choose more user-friendly methods. In Windows XP, for example, you can right-click on a file and select Properties, and then click the Change button on the General tab to open the Open With dialog box (Figure 3.49). From there you can browse to select the program you want to use.

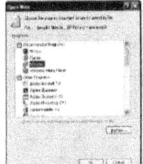

Figure 3.48 Winamp File Settings

Figure 3.49 Changing the file association the easy way

HKEY_CURRENT_USER and HKEY_USERS

Windows is designed to support more than one user on the same PC, storing personalized information such as desktop colours, screensavers, and the contents of the desktop for every user that has an account on the system. HKEY_CURRENT_USER stores the current user settings, and HKEY_USERS stores all of the personalized information for all users on a PC. While you certainly can change items such as the screensaver here, the better way is to right-click on the desktop and select Properties.

HKEY_LOCAL_MACHINE

This root key contains all the data for a system's non-user-specific configurations. This encompasses every device and every program in your PC. For example, Figure 3.50 shows the description of a DVD disc drive.

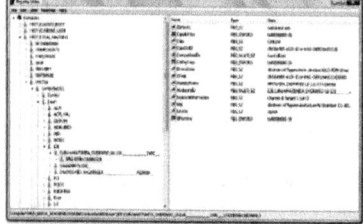

Figure 3.50 Registry information for a DVD drive

HKEY_CURRENT_CONFIG

If the values in HKEY_LOCAL_MACHINE have more than one option, such as two different monitors, this root key defines which one is currently being used. Because most people have only one type of monitor and similar equipment, this area is almost never touched.

Tech Utilities

Windows offers a huge number of utilities that enable techs to configure the OS, optimize and tweak settings, install hardware, and more. The trick is to know where to go to find them. This section shows the six most common locations in Windows where you can access utilities: right-click, Control Panel, System Tools, command line, Administrative Tools, and the Microsoft Management Console. Note that these are locations for tools, not tools themselves, and you can access many tools from more than one of these locations. However, you'll see some of the utilities in many of these locations. Stay sharp in this section, as you'll need to access utilities to understand the inner workings of Windows in the next section.

Right-Click

Windows, being a graphical user interface OS, covers your monitor with windows, menus, icons, file lists all kinds of pretty things you click on to do work. Any single thing you see on your desktop is called an *object*. If you want to open any object in Windows, you double-click on it. If you want to change something about an object, you right-click on it.

Right-clicking on an object brings up a small menu called the *context menu*, and it works on everything in Windows. In fact, try to place your mouse somewhere in Windows where right-clicking does *not* bring up a menu (there are a few places, but they're not easy to find). What you see on the little menu when you right-click varies dramatically depending on the item you decide to right-click. If you right-click a running program in the running program area on the taskbar, you'll see items that relate to a window, such as move, resize, and so on (Figure 3.51). If you right-click on your desktop, you get options for changing the appearance of the desktop (Figure 3.52).

Even different types of files show different results when you right-click on them. Right clicking is something techs do often.

One menu item you'll see almost anywhere you right-click is Properties. Every object in Windows has properties. When you right-click on something and can't find what you're looking for, select Properties. Figure 3.51 shows the results of right-clicking on My Computer? not very exciting. But if you select Properties, you'll get a dialog box like the one shown in Figure 3.52.

Figure 3.51 Right-clicking on a Program

Figure 3.52 Right-clicking on the Desktop

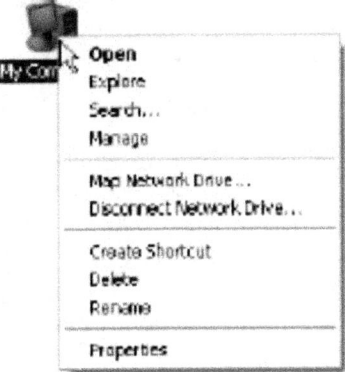

Figure 5.3 Right-clicking on My Computer

Figure 3.54 My Computer Properties
Control Panel

The *Control Panel* handles most of the maintenance, upgrade, and configuration aspects of Windows. As such, the Control Panel is the first set of tools for every tech to explore. Select Start | Settings | Control Panel to open the Control Panel in Windows 2000 and Windows Vista. In Windows XP, the Control Panel is directly on the Start menu by default. The Control Panel in Windows 2000 opens in the traditional icon-littered view. In Windows XP and Vista, the Control Panel opens in the Category view, in which all of the icons are grouped into broad categories such as "Printers and Other Hardware." This view requires an additional click (and sometimes a guess about which category includes the icon you need), so most techs use the Switch to Classic View link to get back to the icons. Figure 3-63 shows the Windows XP Control Panel in both Category and Classic views.

A large number of programs, called *applets*, populate the Control Panel. The names and selection of applets vary depending on the version of Windows and whether any installed programs have added applets. But all versions of Windows share many of the same applets, including Display/Personalization, Add or Remove Programs/Programs and Features, and System (all versions)what I call the *Big Three* applets for techs. With Display/Personalization, you can make changes to the look and feel of your Windows desktop and tweak your video settings. Add or Remove Programs/Programs and Features enables you to add or remove programs. The System applet gives you access to essential system information and tools, such as the Device Manager, although Microsoft wisely added Device Manager right on the Control Panel starting with Vista.

Every icon you see in the Control Panel is actually a file with the extension .CPL.

Any time you get an error opening the Control Panel, you can bet you have a corrupted CPL file. These are a pain to fix. You have to rename all of your CPL files with another extension (I use .CPB) and then rename them back to .CPL one at a time, each time reopening the Control Panel, until you find the CPL file that's causing the lockup.

You can use the Control Panel applets to do an amazing array of things to a Windows system, and each applet displays text that helps explain its functions. The Add Hardware applet in Windows XP, for example, says quite clearly, "Installs and troubleshoots hardware" (Figure 3.54). They are all like that. Figure 3.55 shows the User Accounts applet. Can you determine its use?

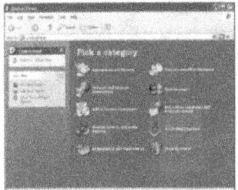

Figure 3.55: Windows XP Control Panel in two views: Category (left) and Classic (right)

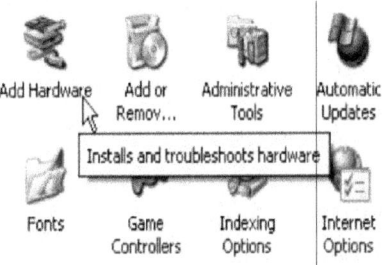

Figure 3.56 Add Hardware Wizard of the Add Hardware applet

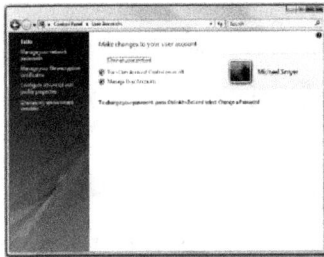

Figure 3.57 User Accounts window of the User Accounts applet

Device Manager

With the *Device Manager*, you can examine and configure all of the hardware and drivers in a Windows PC. As you might suspect from that description, every tech spends a lot of time with this tool! You'll work with the Device Manager many more times during the course of this book and your career as a PC tech. There are many ways to get to the Device Manager—make sure you know all of them!

The first way is to open the Control Panel and double-click the System applet icon. This brings up the System Properties dialog box. In 2000/XP, you access the Device Manager by selecting the Hardware tab and then clicking the Device Manager button. Figure 3.58 shows the Hardware tab of the System Properties dialog box in Windows XP. In Vista/7, the System dialog box has a direct connection to Device Manager (Figure 3.60).

You can also get to the System Properties dialog box in all versions of Windows by right-clicking My Computer/ Computer and selecting Properties. From there, the path to the Device Manager is the same as when you access this dialog box from the Control Panel.

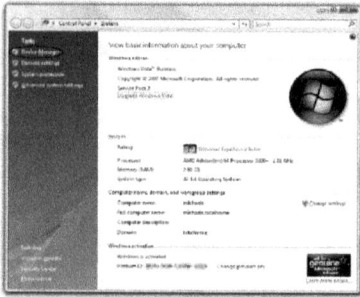

Figure 3.58 Windows XP System applet with the Hardware tab selected

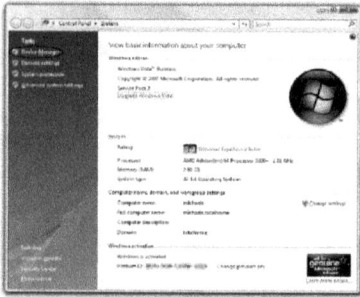

Figure 3.59 Windows Vista System applet with the Device Manager menu option circled

NOTE Holding down the WINDOWS key and pressing PAUSE is yet another way to get to the System Properties dialog box. Keyboard shortcuts are cool! The second (and more streamlined) method is to right-click My Computer/Computer and select Manage. This opens a window called Computer Management, where you'll see Device Manager listed on the left side of the screen, under System Tools. Just click on Device Manager and it opens. You can also access Computer Management by opening the Administrative Tools applet in the Control Panel and then selecting Computer Management (Figure 3.60).

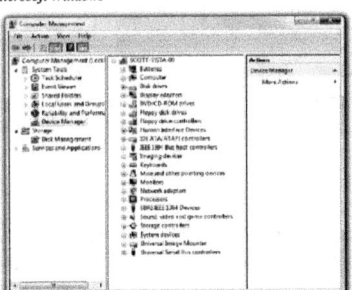

Figure 3.60 Device Manager in Computer Management.

Why are there so many ways to open Device Manager? Well, remember that we're only looking at locations in Windows from which to open utilities, not at the actual utilities themselves. Microsoft wants you to get to the tools you need when you need them, and it's better to have multiple paths to a utility rather than just one.

The Device Manager displays every device that Windows recognizes, organized in special groups called *types*. All devices of the same type are grouped under the same type heading. To see the devices of a particular type, you must open that type's group. Figure 3.60 shows a Windows Vista Device Manager screen with all installed devices in good order? which makes us techs happy. If Windows detects a problem, the device has a red *X* or a black exclamation point on a yellow field, as in the case of the device in Figure 3.61.

Note There is one other "problem" icon you might see on a device in Device Manager a blue *i* on a white field. According to Microsoft, this means you turned off automatic configuration for a device.

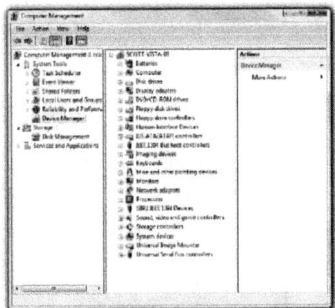

Figure 3.67 Problem device

A red *X* in Windows 2000 or XP means Windows (or you) disabled the deviceright-click on the device to enable it. The tough one is the black exclamation point. If you see this, right-click on the device and select Properties. Read the error code in the Device Status pane, and then look up Microsoft Knowledge Base article 310123 to see what to do. There are around 40 different errorsnobody bothers to memorize them!

(The knowledge base article is for Windows XP, but these error codes are the same in all versions of Windows.) Vista and Windows 7 use the same icons and add one very handy one. If a device is working but you manually disable it, you get a down-arrow (Figure 3.60). Just as in previous versions, right-click the down-arrow and select Properties. You'll see a nice dialog box explaining the issue (Figure 3.61).

The Device Manager isn't just for dealing with problems. It also enables you to update drivers with a simple click of the mouse (assuming you have a replacement driver on your computer.) Right-click a device and select Update Driver from the menu to get the process started. Figure 3.62 shows the options in Windows Vista.

Figure 3.62 Hmm…could be a problem

Figure 3.63 Problem device properties

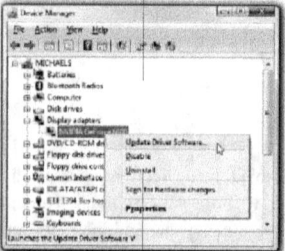

Figure 3.64 Selecting Update Driver Software in the Windows Vista Device Manager

Make sure you can get to Device Manager! You will come back to it again and again in subsequent chapters, because it is the first tool you should access when you have a hardware problem.

System Tools

The Start menu offers a variety of tech utilities collected in one place: select Start | Programs | Accessories | System Tools. In the *System Tools* menu, you'll find commonly accessed tools such as System Information and Disk Defragmenter (Figure 3.65).

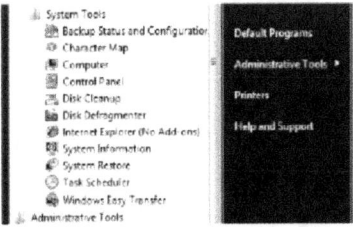

Figure 3-.65   System Tools menu options

Many techs overlook memorizing how to find the appropriate Windows tool to diagnose problems, but nothing hurts your credibility with a client like fumbling around, clicking a variety of menus and applets, while mumbling.

Activate Windows (XP, Vista)

Windows XP unveiled a copy-protection scheme called *activation*. Activation is a process where your computer sends Microsoft a unique code generated on your machine based on the Install CD/DVD's product key and a number of hardware features, such as the amount of RAM, the CPU processor model, and other ones and zeros in your PC. Normally, activation is done at install time, but if you choose not to activate at install or if you make "substantial" changes to the hardware, you'll need to use the Activate Windows utility (Figure 3.65). With the Activate Windows utility, you can activate over the Internet or over the telephone.

Note Once you've activated Windows, this applet goes away.

Backup (2000, XP)

The Backup utility enables you to back up selected files and folders to removable media such as tape drives.

Note Neither Windows XP Home nor Windows XP Media Centre Edition includes Backup during installation. You must install the Backup program from the Windows installation CD by running the \Valueadd\MSFT\Ntbackup\NTbackup.msi program.

Backup Status and Configuration (Vista, 7)

Vista and 7 do not enable you to back up files on your computer selectively. You can only back up personal data with the Backup Status and Configuration Tool or, if you have Vista Business, Ultimate, or Enterprise, perform a complete PC backup by using Windows Complete PC Backup. If you want to pick and choose the file to back up, you need to buy a third-party tool. Also, this tool only allows you to back up to optical media, a hard drive, or a networked drive.

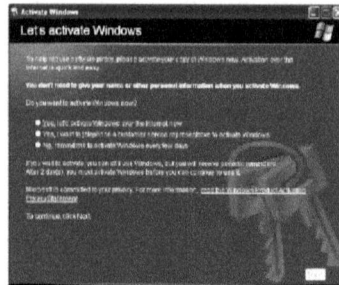

Figure 3.66 Activate Windows

Character Map (All)

Ever been using a program only to discover you need to enter a strange character such as the naira character (N) but your word processor doesn't support it? That's when you need the Character Map. It enables you to copy any Unicode character into the Clipboard (Figure 3.67).

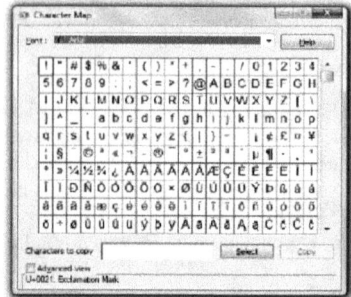

Figure 3.67 Character Map

Disk Cleanup (All)

Disk Cleanup looks for unneeded files on your computer, which is handy when your hard drive starts to get full and you need space. You must run Disk Cleanup manually in Windows 2000, but Windows XP and Windows Vista start this program whenever your hard drive gets below 200 MB of free disk space.

Disk Defragmenter (All)

You use Disk Defragmenter to make your hard drive run faster—you'll see more details on this handy tool in Chapter 12, "Implementing Hard Drives." You can access this utility in the same way you access the Device Manager; you also find Disk Defragmenter in the Computer Management Console. A simpler method is to select Start | All Programs | Accessories | System Tools—you'll find Disk Defragmenter listed there. You can also right-click on any drive in My Computer or Computer, select Properties, and click the Tools tab, where you'll find a convenient Defragment Now button.

Files and Settings Transfer Wizard (Windows XP)

Suppose you have an old computer full of files and settings, and you just bought yourself a brand new computer. You want to copy everything from your old computer onto your new computer? What to do? Microsoft touts the Files and Settings Transfer Wizard as just the tool you need (Figure 3.68). This utility copies your desktop files and folders and,

Figure 3.68 Files and Settings Transfer Wizard (Windows XP)

Character Map most conveniently, your settings from Internet Explorer and Outlook Express; however, it won't copy over your programs, not even the Microsoft ones, and it won't copy settings for any programs other than IE and Outlook Express. If you need to copy everything from an old computer to a new one, you'll probably want to use a disk-imaging tool such as Norton Ghost.

Windows Easy Transfer (Windows Vista)

Vista's Windows Easy Transfer is an aggressively updated version of the Files and Settings Transfer Wizard. It does everything the older version does and adds the capability to copy user accounts and other settings (Figure 3.69).

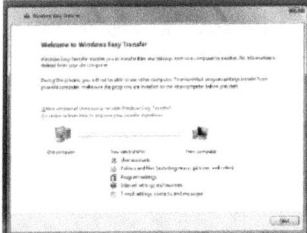

Fig. 3.69: Windows Easy Transfer

Figure 3.70 Scheduled Tasks (All)

With the Scheduled Tasks utility, you can schedule any program to start and stop any time you wish. The only trick to this utility is that you must enter the program you want to run as a command on the command line, with all the proper switches. Figure 3.70 shows the configuration line for running the Disk Defragmenter program.

Security Centre (Windows XP)
The Security Centre is a one-stop location for configuring many security features on your computer. This tool is also in the Control Panel. Vista removes Security Centre from System Tools. All of these security features, and many more, are discussed in detail in their related chapters.

System Information (All)
System Information is one of those tools that everyone likes to talk about, but it's uncommon to meet techs who say they actually use this tool. System Information shows tons of information about the hardware and software on your PC (Figure 3.71). You can also click on the Tools menu to use it as a launch point for a number of programs.

Figure 3.71 System Information (All)

System Restore (XP, Vista)
System Restore is not only handy; it's also arguably the most important single utility you'll ever use

in Windows when it comes to fixing a broken system. System Restore enables you to take a "snapshot"a copy of a number of critical files and settingsand return to that state later (Figure 3.72). System Restore holds multiple snapshots, any of which you may restore to in the future. Imagine you're installing some new device in your PC, or maybe a piece of software. Before you actually install, you take a snapshot and call it "Before Install." You install the device, and now something starts acting weird. You go back into System Restore and reload the previous snapshot, and the problem goes away. System Restore isn't perfect. It only backs up a few critical items, and it's useless if the computer won't boot, but it's usually the first thing to try when something goes wrong? Assuming, of course, you made a snapshot!

BitLocker (Vista Enterprise and Ultimate)

BitLocker is a tool to encrypt files, folders, or entire hard drives. It's a great way to make sure other people can't read your stuff, but it also makes data recovery risky. If you really want security, use BitLocker.

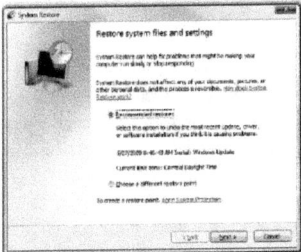

Figure 3.72 System Restore

Command Line

The Windows command-line interface is a throwback to how Microsoft operating systems worked a long, long time ago when text commands were entered at a command prompt. Figure 3.73 shows the command prompt from DOS, the first operating system commonly used in Pcs.

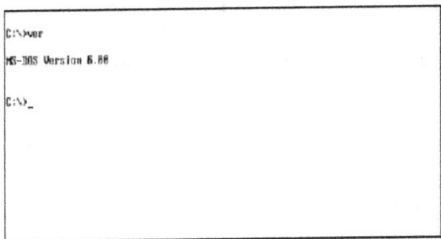

Figure 3.73 DOS Command Prompt

Note The command-line interface goes back to the early days of computing, but it continues to be an essential tool in all modern operating systems, including Linux, Mac OS X, and all versions of Windows. "Working with the Command-Line Interface," goes into the command line in detail. DOS is dead, but the command-line interface is alive and well in every version of Windows? Including Windows 7. Every good tech knows how to access and use the command-line interface. It is a lifesaver when the graphical part of Windows doesn't work, and it is often faster than using a mouse if you're skilled at using it. An entire chapter is devoted to the command line, but let's look at one example of what the command line can do. First, you need to get there. In Windows XP, select Start | Run, and type **cmd** in the dialog box. Click OK and you get to a command prompt. In Windows Vista, you do the same thing in the Start | Start Search dialog box. Figure 3.74 shows a command prompt in Windows Vista.

Figure 3.74 Command Prompt in Windows Vista

Once at a command prompt, type **dir** and press ENTER on your keyboard. This command displays all the files and folders in a specific directoryprobably your user folder for this exerciseand gives sizes and other information. DIR is just one of many useful command-line tools you'll learn about in this book.

Microsoft Management Console

One of the biggest complaints about earlier versions of Windows was the wide dispersal of the many utilities needed for administration and troubleshooting. Despite years of research, Microsoft could never find a place for all the utilities that would please even a small minority of support people. In a moment of sheer genius, Microsoft determined that the ultimate utility was one that the support people made for themselves! This brought on the creation of the amazing Microsoft Management Console.

The *Microsoft Management Console* (*MMC*) is simply a shell program in Windows that holds individual utilities called *snap-ins*. To start an MMC, select Start | Run or just Start, type **mmc** and press ENTER to get a blank MMC. Blank MMCs aren't much to look at (Figure 3.75).

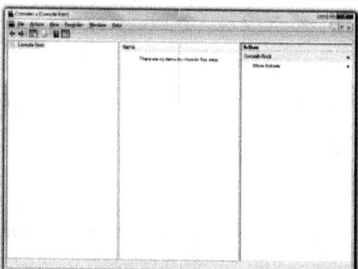

Figure 3.75 Blank MMC

You make a blank MMC console useful by adding snap-ins, which include most of the utilities you use in Windows. Even the good old Device Manager is a snap-in. You can add as many snap-ins as you like, and you have many to choose from. Many companies sell third-party utilities as MMC snap-ins.

For example, to add the Device Manager snap-in, open the blank MMC and select File | Add/ Remove Snap-in (Console |Add/Remove Snap-in in Windows 2000). Here you will see a list of available snap-ins in Windows Vista (Figure 3.76). (Click the Add button in 2000/XP to open a similar screen.) Select Device Manager, and click the Add button to open a dialog box that prompts you to choose the local or a remote PC for the snap-in to work with. Choose Local Computer for this exercise, and click the Finish button. Click the Close button to close the Add Standalone Snap-in dialog box, and then click OK to close the Add/Remove Snap-in dialog box.

You should see Device Manager listed in the console. Click it. Hey, that looks kind of familiar, doesn't it (see Figure 3.77)?

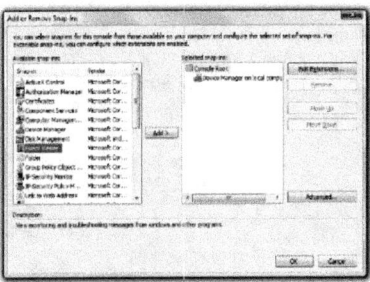

Figure 3.76 Available snap-ins

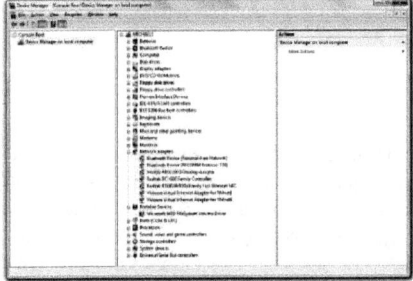

Figure 3.77 Device Manager as a snap-in

Once you've added the snap-ins you want, just save the console under any name, anywhere you want. I'll save this console as Device Manager, for example, and drop it on my desktop (see Figure 3-86). I'm now just a double-click away from the Device Manager.

Figure 3.78 The Device Manager shortcut on the desktop

Administrative Tools

Windows combines the most popular snap-ins into an applet in the Control Panel called *Administrative Tools*. Open the Control Panel and open Administrative Tools (Figure 3.79). Administrative Tools is really just a folder that stores a number of pre-made consoles. As you poke through these, notice that many of the consoles share some of the same snap-ins—nothing wrong with that. Of the consoles in a standard Administrative Tools collection, the ones you'll spend the most time with are Computer Management, Event Viewer, Reliability and Performance (or just Performance in Windows 2000/XP), and Services.

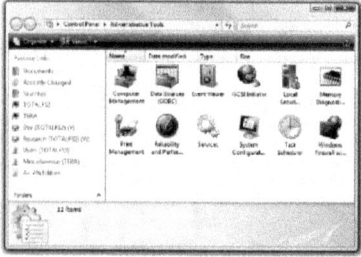

Figure 3.79 Administrative Tools

Computer Management

The *Computer Management* applet is a tech's best buddy, or at least a place where you'll spend a lot of time when building or maintaining a system (Figure 3.80). You've already spent considerable time with two of its components: System Tools and Storage. Depending on the version of Windows, System Tools also offers System Information, Performance Logs and Alerts, Reliability and Performance, Device Manager, and more. Storage is where you'll find Disk Management.

Event Viewer

Event Viewer shows you at a glance what has happened in the last day, week, or more, including when people logged in and when the PC had problems (Figure 3.81).

Performance (Windows 2000/XP)

The *Performance* console consists of two snap-ins: System Monitor and Performance Logs and Alerts. You can use these for reading *logs* files that record information over time. The System

Monitor can also monitor real-time data (Figure 3.82).

Suppose you are adding a new cable modem and you want to know just how fast you can download data. Click the plus sign (+) on the toolbar to add a counter.

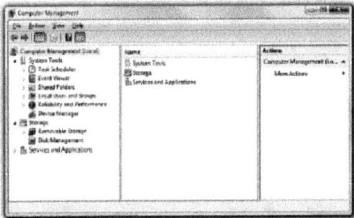

Click Figure 3.80 Computer Management applet

Figure 3.81 Event Viewer reporting system errors

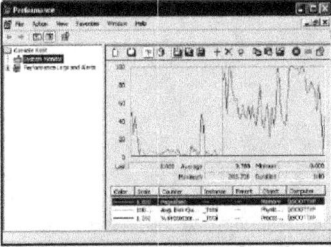

Figure 3.82 System Monitor in action

Setting up a throughput test the *Use local computer counters* radio button, and then choose Network Interface from the Performance Object pull-down menu. Make sure the *Select counters from list* radio button is selected. Last, select Bytes Received/sec. The dialog box should look like Figure 3-91.

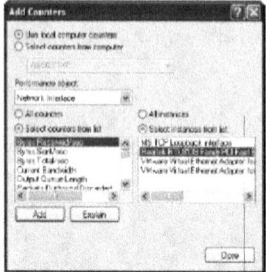

Figure 3.83 Dialog Box

Click Add, and then click Close; probably not much is happening. Go to a Web site, preferably one where you can download a huge file. Start downloading and watch the chart jump; that's the real throughput (Figure 3.84).

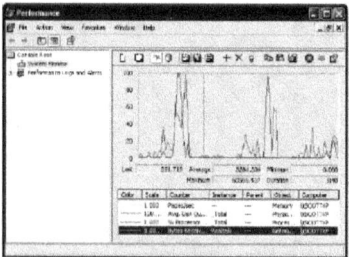

Figure 3.84 Downloading with Blazing Speed

Reliability and Performance Monitor (Windows Vista)

The *Reliability and Performance Monitor* in Windows Vista offers just about everything you can find in the Performance applet of older versions of Windows although everything is monitored by default, so there's no need to add anything. In addition, it includes the Reliability Monitor. The Reliability Monitor enables you to see at a glance what's been done to the computer over a period of time, including software installations and uninstallations, failures of hardware or applications, and general uptime (Figure 3.85). It's a nice starting tool for checking a Vista machine that's new to you.

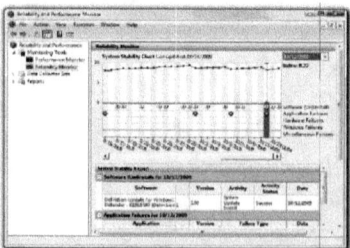

Figure 3.85 The Reliability and Performance Monitor open to the Reliability Monitor screen.

Services

Windows runs a large number of separate programs called *services*. The best way to visualize a service is to think of it as something that runs, yet is invisible. Windows comes with about 100 services by default, and they handle a huge number of tasks, from application support to network functions. You can use the Services applet to see the status of all services on the system, including services that are not running (Figure 3.86). Right-click a service and select Properties to modify its settings. Figure 3.87 shows the properties for the Bluetooth support service. See the Startup type pull-down menu? It shows three options: Automatic, Manual, and Disabled. Automatic means it starts when the system starts, Manual means you have to come to this tab to start it, and Disabled prevents anything from starting it. Make sure you know these three settings, and also make sure you understand how to start, stop, pause, and resume services (note the our buttons below Startup Type).

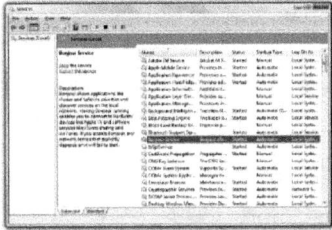

Figure 3.86 Services Applet

Windows 7

Windows 7 came out just a few months after CompTIA announced the 220-701 and 220-702 exams, so it's not on those exams. However, the differences between Vista and 7 are so minor "under the hood" that it's safe to say if you know Vista, you know Windows 7 (Figure 3.88).

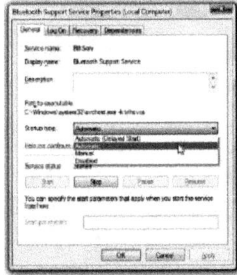

Figure 3.87 Bluetooth Support Service Properties

Figure 3.88 Windows 7

Windows Mobile

Windows Mobile is a very small version of Windows designed for PDAs and phones. Windows Mobile is only available as an Original Equipment Manufacturer (OEM) product, which means you buy the device and it comes with Windows Mobile you can't buy some PDA or phone and then buy Windows Mobile separately.

Windows XP Tablet PC Edition

A tablet PC is a laptop with a built-in touch screen. The idea behind a tablet PC is to drastically reduce, if not totally eliminate, the use of a keyboard (Figure 3.89). In some situations, tablet PCs have started to become popular. Windows XP Tablet PC Edition is Microsoft's operating solution for tablet PCs. Tablet PC Edition is still Windows XP, but it adds special drivers and applications to support the tablet.

REVISION QUESTION

1. Which utility is helpful in troubleshooting hardware?
    A. Security Centre   B. System Properties
    C. Disk Management   D. Device Manager

2. Which utility is missing from the default Windows XP Home installation?
    A. Computer Management B. Character Map
    C. User Accounts   D.   Backup

3. What is displayed in the My Computer window?
    A. Installed programs   B. All the Control Panel applets
    C. All the drives on your system D. Other computers on the network

4. What folder is a central storage location for user files in XP?
    A. My Files   B. My Documents
    C. Program Files   D. %Systemroot%\Users

5. Which version of Windows uses the Backup Status and Configuration Tool?
    A. Windows Vista Ultimate B. Windows XP Media Centre
    C. Windows XP Professional   D.   Windows 2000

6. Which of the following is an advantage of running Windows on NTFS as opposed to FAT?
    A. Long filenames   B. Multiple folders
    C. Speed   D. Security

CHAPTER FOUR

PREVENTIVE MAINTENANCE
AND TROUBLESHOOTING

4.1   INTRODUCTION

This chapter introduces preventive maintenance and the troubleshooting process. *Preventive maintenance* is a regular and systematic inspection, cleaning, and replacement of worn parts, materials, and systems. Preventive maintenance helps to prevent failure of parts, materials, and systems by ensuring that they are in good working order. *Troubleshooting* is a systematic approach to locating the cause of a fault in a computer system. A good preventive maintenance program helps minimize failures. With fewer failures, there is a less troubleshooting to do, thus saving an organization's time and money. Preventive maintenance can also include upgrading certain hardware or software such as a hard drive that is making noise, upgrading memory that is insufficient, or installing software updates for security or reliability.

Troubleshooting is a learnt skill. Not all troubleshooting processes are the same, and technicians tend to refine their troubleshooting skills based on knowledge and personal experience.
Use the guidelines in this chapter as a starting point to help develop your troubleshooting skills. Although each situation is different, the process described in this chapter will help you to determine your course of action when you are trying to solve a technical problem for a customer.

4.2   THE PURPOSE OF PREVENTIVE MAINTENANCE

Preventive maintenance is used to reduce the probability of hardware or software problems by systematically and periodically checking hardware and software to ensure proper operation.

Check the condition of cables, components, and peripherals. Clean components to reduce the likelihood of overheating. Repair or replace components that show signs of abuse or excess wear. Use the following tasks as a guide to create a hardware maintenance program:

♦   Remove dust from fan intakes.

♦   Check and secure loose cables.

♦   Remove dust from components inside the computer.

♦   Clean the mouse and keyboard.

♦   Remove dust from the power supply.

Verify that installed software is current. Follow the policies of the organization when installing security updates, operating system updates, and program updates. Many organizations do not allow updates until extensive testing has been completed. This testing is done to confirm that the update will not cause problems with the operating system and software.

Use the tasks listed as a guide to create a software maintenance schedule that fits the needs of your computer equipment:

♦   Review security updates
♦   Defragment hard drives
♦   Review driver updates
♦   Update virus definition files
♦   Review software updates
♦   Scan hard drives for errors
♦   Scan for viruses and spyware
♦   Remove unwanted programs

Be proactive in computer equipment maintenance and data protection. By performing regular maintenance routines, you can reduce potential hardware and software problems. Doing this will reduce computer downtime and repair costs.

A preventive maintenance plan is developed based on the needs of the equipment. A computer exposed to a dusty environment, such as a construction site, will need more attention than equipment in an office environment. High-traffic networks, such as a school network, can require additional scanning and removal of malicious software or unwanted files.

Document the routine maintenance tasks that must be performed on the computer equipment and the frequency of each task. This list of tasks can then be used to create a maintenance program. Remember, the more you use your computer, the more frequently you should perform preventive maintenance. This can include doing a defragmentation of the hard drive weekly rather than monthly, continually scanning files for viruses rather than performing a scan once a week, and checking for updates for software and hardware every two weeks rather than monthly.

Some benefits of preventive maintenance include the following:
♦   Reduces the number of equipment failures
♦   Extends the life of the components
♦   Increases equipment stability
♦   Increases data protection
♦   Reduces repair costs

4.3 THE STEPS OF THE TROUBLESHOOTING PROCESS
Troubleshooting requires an organized and logical approach to problems with computers and other components. A logical approach to troubleshooting allows you to eliminate variables in a systematic order. Asking the right questions, testing the right hardware, and examining the right data help you understand the problem. This helps you form a proposed solution.
Troubleshooting is a skill that you will refine over time. Each time you solve another problem, you will increase your troubleshooting skills by gaining more experience. You will learn how and when to combine, as well as skip, steps to reach a solution quickly. The troubleshooting process is a guideline that you can modify to fit your needs.

In the following sections, you will learn an approach to problem solving that you can apply to both hardware and software. You also can apply many of the steps to problem solving in other work-related areas.

The troubleshooting process consists of the following steps:

Step 1. Gather data from the customer.

Step 2. Verify the obvious.

Step 3. Try quick or less intensive solutions first.

Step 4. Gather data from the computer.

Step 5. Evaluate the problem and implement the solution.

Step 6. Close with the customer.

It is best to follow this process and document the process as you go through it. This will help you to identify solutions the next time you encounter a similar problem and help you work backward if you made unwanted changes.

Note: The term *customer*, as used in this course, is any user that requires technical computer assistance.

After completing the following sections, you will be able to explain the purpose of data protection and perform each step in the troubleshooting process.

4.4　EXPLAIN THE PURPOSE OF DATA PROTECTION

Before you begin troubleshooting problems, always follow the necessary precautions to protect data on a computer. Some repairs, such as replacing a hard drive or reinstalling an operating system, can put the data on the computer at risk. Make sure that you do everything possible to prevent data loss while attempting repairs.

Caution

Although data protection is not one of the six troubleshooting steps, you must protect data before beginning any work on a customer's computer. If your work results in data loss for the customer, you or your company could be held liable.

A ***backup*** is a copy of the data on a computer hard drive that is saved to media such as a CD, DVD, or tape drive. In an organization, backups are routinely done on a daily, weekly, and monthly basis.

How To

If you are unsure that a backup has been done, do not attempt any troubleshooting activities until you check with the customer. Here is a list of items to verify with the customer about data backups:

♦　Date of the last backup

♦　Data integrity of the backup

♦　Availability of all backup media for a data restore

♦　Contents of the backup

If the customer does not have a current backup and you are not able to create one, you should ask the customer to sign a liability release form. A liability release form should contain at least the following information:

♦   Permission to work on the computer without a current backup available

♦   Release from liability if data is lost or corrupted

♦   Description of the work to be performed

4.5   GATHERING DATA FROM THE CUSTOMERS

During the troubleshooting process, gather as much information from the customer as possible. The customer will provide you with the basic facts about the problem. Here is a list of some of the important information to gather from the customer:

♦   Customer information

♦   Computer configuration

♦   Manufacturer and model

♦   Operating system information

♦   Network environment

♦   Connection type

♦   Description of problem

♦   Open-ended questions

♦   Company name

♦   Contact name

♦   Address

♦   Phone number

♦   Closed-ended questions

When you are talking to the customer, you should follow these guidelines:

♦   Ask direct questions to gather information.

♦   Do not talk down to the customer.

♦   Do not insult the customer.

♦   Do not use the industry jargon when talking to customers.

♦   Do not accuse the customer of causing the problem.

By communicating effectively, you will be able to elicit the most relevant information about the problem from the customer.

When gathering information from customers, use both open-ended and closed-ended questions. Start with ***open-ended questions*** to obtain general information. Open-ended questions allow customers to explain the details of the problem in their own words. Some examples of open-ended questions are

♦   What problems are you experiencing with your computer or network?

♦   What software has been installed on your computer recently?

♦   What were you doing when the problem was identified?

♦   What hardware changes have recently been made to your computer?

Based on the information from the customer, you can proceed with closed-ended questions.

Closed-ended questions generally requires a yes or no answer. These questions are intended to get the most relevant information in the shortest possible time. Some examples of closed ended questions are

♦ Has anyone else used your computer recently?

♦ Can you reproduce the problem?

♦ Are you currently logged in to the network?

♦ Have you received any error messages on your computer?

♦ Have you changed your password recently?

The information obtained from the customer should be documented in the work order and in the repair journal. The work order is a record of what was done and the time that it took to make the repair. The repair journal is a written record of anything that was learned during the repair that can help you on future projects. Write down anything that you think might be important for you or another technician. Often, the small details can lead to the solution of a difficult problem.

Verify the Obvious Issues

The second step in the troubleshooting process is to verify the obvious issues. Even though the customer might think that there is a major problem, start with the obvious issues before moving to more complex diagnoses.

Verify the following obvious issues:

♦ Loose external cable connections.

♦ Non bootable disk in floppy drive.

♦ Power switch for an outlet is turned off.

♦ Incorrect boot order in BIOS.

♦ Surge protector is turned off.

♦ Device is powered off.

If you find an obvious issue that fixes the problem, you can go to the last step and close with the customer. These steps are simply a guideline to help you solve problems in an efficient manner. If the problem is not resolved when you verify the obvious issues, you will need to continue with the troubleshooting process.

Try Quick Solutions First

The next step in the troubleshooting process is to try quick solutions first. Obvious issues and quick solutions sometimes overlap each other and can be used together to repair the problem. Document each solution that you try. Information about the solutions that you have tried is vital if the problem needs to be escalated to another technician.

Some common quick solutions include

♦ Log in as a different user.

♦ Check that all cables are connected to the proper ports.

♦ Remove and reconnect cables.

♦ Reboot the computer or network device.

♦   Check computer for the latest OS patches and updates.

If a quick solution does not resolve the problem, document your results and try the next most likely solution. Continue this process until you have solved the problem or have tried all the quick solutions. Document the resolution for future reference.

Gather Data from the Computer

The next step in the troubleshooting process is to gather data from the computer. You have tried all the quick solutions, but the problem is still not resolved. It is now time to verify the customer's description of the problem by gathering data from the computer.

To help gather information from the computer, you will need to be aware of some of the most common utilities or features of a computer. These utilities or features include the Event Viewer, Device Manager, BIOS information and beep codes, and various diagnostic tools.

4.6   EVENT VIEWER

When system, user, or software errors occur on a computer, the *Event Viewer* is updated with information about the errors. The Event Viewer application, shown in Figure 4.1, records the following information about the problem:

♦   The problem that occurred

♦   The source of the problem

♦   The severity of the problem

♦   The date and time of the problem

♦   Event ID number

♦   The user who was logged in when the problem occurred

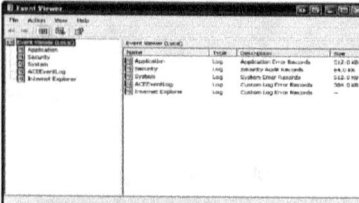

Figure 4.1 Event Viewer

Although this utility lists, give details about the error, you might still need to research the solution.

4.7   DEVICE MANAGER

The *Device Manager*, shown in Figure 4-2, displays all the devices that are configured on a computer. Any device that the operating system determines to be acting incorrectly will be flagged with an error icon. This type of error is denoted as a yellow circle with an exclamation point (!). If a device is disabled, it will be flagged with a red circle and an X.

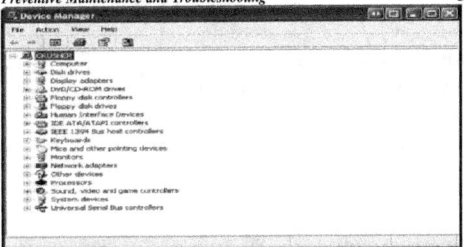

Figure 4.2 Device Manager

Each BIOS manufacturer has a unique beep sequence for hardware failures. When troubleshooting, power on the computer and then listen. As the system proceeds through the *power-on self test (POST)*, most computers will emit one beep to indicate that the system is booting properly. If there is an error, you might hear multiple beeps. Document the beep code sequence, and research the code to determine the specific hardware failure.

BIOS Information If the computer boots and stops after the POST, you should investigate the BIOS settings to determine where to find the problem. A device might not be detected or configured properly. Refer to the motherboard manual to make sure that the BIOS settings are accurate.

4.8   DIAGNOSTIC TOOLS

Conduct research to determine what software is available to help diagnose and solve problems. There are many programs available that can help you troubleshoot hardware. Often, manufacturers of system hardware provide their own diagnostic tools. A hard drive manufacturer, for example, might provide a tool that can be used to boot the computer and diagnose problems with the hard drive when it will not start Windows.

Evaluate the Problem and Implement the Solution

The next step in the troubleshooting process is to evaluate the problem and implement the solution. When researching possible solutions for a problem, use the following sources of information:

♦   Your own problem-solving experience

♦   Other technicians

♦   Internet search

♦   Device manuals

♦   Online forums

♦   Newsgroups

♦   Manufacturer FAQs

♦   Computer manuals

♦   Technical websites

Divide larger problems into smaller problems that you can analyze and solve individually. You should prioritize solutions, starting with the easiest and fastest to implement. Create a list of possible solutions and implement them one at a time. If you implement a possible solution and it does not work, reverse the solution and try another.

Close with the Customer

After the repairs to the computer have been completed, finish the troubleshooting process by closing with the customer. Communicate the problem and the solution to the customer verbally and in all documentation. The steps to be taken when you have finished a repair and are closing with the customer include

♦ Discuss the solution implemented with the customer.
♦ Have the customer verify that the problem has been solved.
♦ Provide the customer with all paperwork.
♦ Document the steps taken to solve the problem in the work order and in the technician's journal.
♦ Document any components used in the repair.
♦ Document the amount of time spent to resolve the problem.

Verify the solution with the customer. If the customer is available, demonstrate how the solution has corrected the computer problem. Have the customer test the solution and try to reproduce the problem. When the customer can verify that the problem has been resolved, you can complete the documentation for the repair in the work order and in your journal.
The documentation should include the following information:

♦ The description of the problem
♦ The steps to resolve the problem
♦ The components used in the repair

Summary in Preventing Maintenance and Troubleshooting
This chapter discussed the concepts of preventive maintenance and the troubleshooting process, including the following important points:

♦ Regular preventive maintenance reduces hardware and software problems.

♦ Before beginning any repair, back up the data on a computer.

♦ The troubleshooting process is a guideline to help you solve computer problems in an efficient manner.

REVISION QUESTIONS

1. What is the last step in the troubleshooting process?
    A. Verify the obvious issues.   B. Gather data from the customer.
    C. Try quick solutions.
    D. Evaluate the problem and implement the solution.
    E. Close with the customer.
    F. Gather data from the computer.

2. Which type of question allows the customer to completely describe the problem?

    A. Closed-ended B. Open-ended C. Technical D. Specific
3. Which of the following common tasks are performed during preventive maintenance?
    A. Update drivers.   B. Update the RAM.
    C. Install additional peripherals.   D. Check and secure loose cables.
    E. Reinstall the operating system. F. Clean the mouse and keyboard.

CHAPTER FIVE

PRINCIPLES OF NETWORKING

5.1   INTRODUCTION

This chapter provides an overview of Principles of Networking.

The following types of networks are discussed in this chapter:

- Local-area network (LAN)
- Wide-area network (WAN)
- Wireless LAN (WLAN)

This chapter discusses the different types of network topologies, protocols, and logical models as well as the hardware needed to create a network. Configuration, troubleshooting, and preventive maintenance also are covered. In addition, you will learn about network software, communication methods, and hardware relationships.

5.2   PRINCIPLES OF NETWORKING

Networks are systems that are formed by links. Websites that allow individuals to link to each other's pages are called social networking sites. A set of related ideas can be called a conceptual network. The connections you have with all your friends can be called your personal network. People use the following networks every day:

- The Internet
- Mail delivery system
- Corporate computer network
- Public transportation system
- Telephone system

Computers can be linked by networks to share data and resources. A network can be as simple as two computers connected by a single cable or as complex as hundreds of computers connected to devices that control the flow of information. Converged data networks can include general-purpose computers, such as PCs and servers, as well as devices with more specific functions, including printers, phones, televisions, and game consoles. All data, voice, video, and converged networks share information and use various methods to direct how this information flows. The information on the network goes from one place to another, sometimes via different paths, to arrive at the appropriate destination. The public transportation system is similar to a data network. The cars, trucks, and other vehicles are like the messages that travel within the network. Each driver defines a starting point (source) and an ending point (destination). Within this system are rules such as stop signs and traffic lights that control the flow from the source to the destination. After completing this section, you will meet these objectives:

- Define computer networks.
- The benefits of networking.

5.3   DEFINITION OF COMPUTER NETWORKS

A computer network is a collection of hosts connected by *networking* devices. A host is any device that sends and receives information on the network. Peripherals are devices that are connected to hosts. Some devices can serve as either hosts or peripherals. For example, a printer connected to your laptop that is on a network is acting as a peripheral. If the printer is connected directly to a networking device, such as a hub, switch, or router, it is acting as a host. Computer networks are used globally in schools, homes, businesses and government agencies. Many of these networks are connected to each other through the Internet. Many different types of devices can connect to a network:

- Laptop computers
- Desktop computers
- Scanners
- Printers
- PDAs
- Smartphones
- File/print servers

A network can share many different types of resources:

- Services, such as printing or scanning
- Storage space on removable devices, such as hard drives or optical drives
- Applications, such as databases

You can use networks to access information stored on other computers, print documents using shared printers, and synchronize the calendar between your computer and your Smartphone. Network devices are linked using a variety of connections:

- **Copper cabling** uses electrical signals to transmit data between devices.

- **Fiber-optic cabling** uses glass or plastic wire, also called fiber, to carry information as light pulses.

- **Wireless connection** uses radio signals, infrared technology (laser), or satellite transmissions.

5.4   THE BENEFITS OF NETWORKING

The benefits of networking computers and other devices include lower costs and increased productivity. With networks, resources can be shared, which results in less duplication and me benefits of using networks:

- **Fewer Peripherals are Needed:** Figure 5.1 shows that many devices can be connected on a network. Each computer on the network does not need its own printer, scanner, or backup device. Multiple printers can be set up in a central location and can be shared among the network users. All network users send print jobs to a central print server that manages the print requests. The print server can distribute print jobs over multiple printers or can queue jobs that require a specific printer.

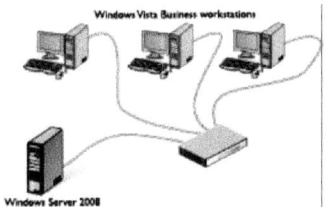

Figure 5.1 Shared Resources

- **Increased Communication Capabilities:** Networks provide several different collaboration tools that can be used to communicate between network users. Online collaboration tools include e-mail, forums and chats, voice and video, and instant messaging. With these tools, users can communicate with friends, family, and colleagues.

- **Avoid File Duplication and Corruption:** A server manages network resources. Servers store data and share it with users on a network. Confidential or sensitive data can be protected and shared with the users who have permission to access that data. Document-tracking software can be used to prevent users from overwriting files, or changing files that others are accessing at the same time.

- **Lower-cost Licensing:** Application licensing can be expensive for individual computers.

Many software vendors offer site licenses for networks, which can dramatically reduce the cost of software. The site license allows a group of people or an entire organization to use the application for a single fee.

- **Centralized Administration:** Centralized administration reduces the number of people needed to manage the devices and data on the network, reducing time and cost to the company. Individual network users do not need to manage their own data and devices. One administrator can control the data, devices, and permissions of users on the network. Backing up data is easier because the data is stored in a central location.

- **Conserve Resources:** Data processing can be distributed across many computers to prevent one computer from becoming overloaded with processing tasks.

5.5 TYPES OF NETWORKS
Data networks continue to evolve in complexity, use, and design. Different types of networks have different descriptive names. A computer network is identified by the following specific characteristics:
- The area it serves
- How the data is stored
- How the resources are managed
- How the network is organized
- The type of networking devices used

- The type of media used to connect the devices

After completing this section, you will meet these objectives:
- Describe a LAN
- Describe a WAN
- Describe a WLAN
- Explain peer-to-peer networks
- Explain client/server networks

LAN

A Local-Area Network (LAN) is a group of interconnected devices that is under the same administrative control, as shown in Figure 5-2. In the past, LANs were considered to be small networks that existed in a single physical location. Although LANs can be as small as a single local network installed in a home or small office, over time, the definition of LANs has evolved to include interconnected local networks consisting of many hundreds of devices, installed in multiple buildings and locations.

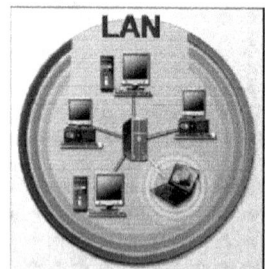

Figure 5.2 Local-Area Network

The important thing to remember is that all the local networks within a LAN are under one administrative control group that governs the security and access control policies that are in force on the network. In this context, the word "local" in local-area network refers to local consistent control rather than being physically close to each other. Devices in a LAN may be physically close, but this is not a requirement.

WAN

Wide-Area Networks (WAN) are networks that connect LANs in geographically separated locations, as shown in Figure 5.3. The most common example of a WAN is the Internet. The Internet is a large WAN that is composed of millions of interconnected LANs. Telecommunications service providers (TSP) are used to interconnect these LANs at different locations.

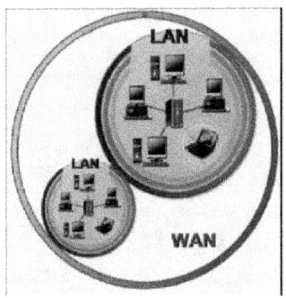

Figure 5.3 Wide-Area Network

WLAN

In a traditional LAN, devices are interconnected using copper cabling. In some environments, installing copper cabling may not be practical, desirable, or even possible. In these situations, wireless devices are used to transmit and receive data using radio waves. These networks are called *wireless LANs (WLAN)*. Figure 5.4 shows a WLAN. As with LANs, on a WLAN you can share resources, such as files and printers, and access the Internet.

Figure 5.4 Wireless Local-Area Network

In a WLAN, wireless devices connect to access points within a specified area. Access points typically are connected to the network using copper cabling. Instead of providing copper cabling to every network host, only the wireless access point is connected to the network with copper cabling. WLAN coverage can be small and limited to the area of a room or can have greater range.

5.6   PEER-TO-PEER NETWORKS

In a *peer-to-peer network*, devices are connected directly to each other without any additional networking devices between them, as shown in Figure 5.5. In this type of network, each device has equivalent capabilities and responsibilities. Individual users are responsible for their own resources and can decide which data and devices to share. Because individual users are responsible for the resources on their own computers, the network has no central point of control or administration.

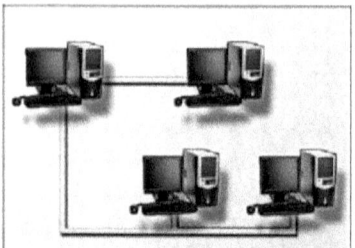

Figure 5.5 Peer-to-Peer Network

Peer-to-peer networks work best in environments with ten or fewer computers. Because individual users are in control of their own computers, there is no need to hire a dedicated network administrator. Peer-to-peer networks have several disadvantages:

♦   They have no centralized network administration, which makes it difficult to determine who controls resources on the network.

♦   They have no centralized security. Each computer must use separate security measures for data protection.

♦   The network becomes more complex and difficult to manage as the number of computers on the network increases.

♦   There may be no centralized data storage. Separate data backups must be maintained. This responsibility falls on the individual users.

Peer-to-peer networks still exist inside larger networks today. Even on a large client network, users can still share resources directly with other users without using a network server. In your home, if you have more than one computer, you can set up a peer-to-peer network. You can share files with other computers, send messages between them, and print documents to a shared printer.

5.7   CLIENT/SERVER NETWORKS

In a *client/server network*, shown in Figure 5-6, the client requests information or services from the server. The server provides the requested information or service to the client. Servers on a client/server network commonly perform some of the processing work for client machines, such as sorting through a database before delivering only the records requested by the client.

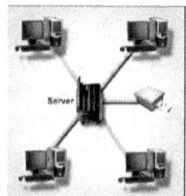

Figure 5.6 Client/Server Network

One example of a client/server network is a corporate environment in which employees use a company e-mail server to send, receive, and store e-mail. The e-mail client on an employee computer issues a request to the e-mail server for any unread e-mail. The server responds by sending the requested e-mail to the client. In a client/server model, the servers are maintained by network administrators. Data backups and security measures are implemented by the network administrator. The network administrator also controls user access to the network resources. All the data on the network is stored on a centralized file server. Shared printers on the network are managed by a centralized print server. Network users with the proper permissions can access both the data and shared printers. Each user must provide an authorized username and password to gain access to network resources that he or she is permitted to use.

For data protection, an administrator performs a routine backup of all the files on the servers. If a computer crashes, or data is lost, the administrator can easily recover the data from a recent backup.

5.8 BASIC NETWORKING CONCEPTS AND TECHNOLOGIES

As a computer technician, you will be required to configure and troubleshoot computers on a network. To effectively configure a computer on the network, you should understand *IP addressing*, *protocols*, and other network concepts.

After completing this section, you will meet these objectives:
♦   Explain bandwidth and data transmission.
♦   Describe IP addressing.
♦   Define DHCP.
♦   Describe Internet protocols and applications.
♦   Define ICMP.

Bandwidth is the amount of data that can be transmitted within a fixed time period. When data is sent over a computer network, it is broken into small chunks called packets. Each packet contains headers. A header is information added to each packet that contains the packet's source and destination. A header also contains information that describes how to put all the packets back together again at the destination. The size of the bandwidth determines the amount of information that can be transmitted.

Bandwidth is measured in bits per second and usually is denoted by any of the following units of measure:
♦   *bps* is bits per second.
♦   *kbps* is kilobits per second.
♦   *Mbps* is megabits per second.

Note
1 byte is equal to 8 bits and is abbreviated with a capital B. 1 MBps is approximately 8 Mbps.

Figure 8.7 shows how bandwidth on a network can be compared to a highway. In this example, the cars and trucks represent the data. The number of lanes on the highway represents the number of cars that can travel on the highway at the same time. An eight-lane highway can handle four times the number of cars that a two-lane highway can.

Figure 5.7 Highway Analogy

The data that is transmitted over the network can flow using one of three modes: simplex, half duplex, or full duplex:

♦   ***Simplex***: Simplex, also called unidirectional, is a single one-way transmission. An example of simplex transmission is the signal that is sent from a TV station to your TV.

♦   ***Half Duplex***: When data flows in one direction at a time, this is known as half duplex. With half duplex, the communications channel allows alternating transmission in two directions, but not in both directions simultaneously. Two-way radios, such as police and emergency communications mobile radios, work with half-duplex transmissions. When you press the button on the microphone to transmit, you cannot hear the person on the other end. If people at both ends try to talk at the same time, neither transmission gets through.

♦   ***Full Duplex***: When data flows in both directions at the same time, this is known as full duplex. Although the data flows in both directions, the bandwidth is measured in only one direction. A network cable with 100 Mbps in full-duplex mode has a bandwidth of 100 Mbps. A telephone conversation is an example of full-duplex communication. Both people can talk and be heard at the same time. Full-duplex networking technology increases network performance because data can be sent and received at the same time. Broadband technology allows multiple signals to travel on the same wire simultaneously. ***Broadband*** technologies, such as ***digital subscriber line (DSL)*** and cable, operate in full-duplex mode. With a DSL connection, for example, users can download data to their computer and talk on the telephone at the same time.

5.9   IP ADDRESSING
An ***IP address*** is a number that is used to identify a device on the network. Each device on a network must have a unique IP address to communicate with other network devices. As noted earlier, a host is a device that sends or receives information on the network. Network devices are devices that move data across the network, including hubs, switches, and routers. On a LAN, each host and network device must have an IP address within the same network to be able to communicate with each other.

A person's name and fingerprints usually do not change. They provide a label or address for the person's physical aspect the body. A person's mailing address, on the other hand, relates to where the person lives or picks up mail. This address can change. On a host, the Media Access Control (MAC) address (explained in the section "Manual Configuration") is assigned to the host NIC and is known as the physical address. The physical address remains the same regardless of where the host is placed on the network in the same way that fingerprints remain with someone regardless of where she goes. The IP address is similar to someone's mailing address. It is known as a logical address because it is logically assigned based on the host location. The IP address, or network address, is based on the local network and is assigned to each host by a network administrator.

This process is similar to the local government assigning a street address based on the logical description of the city or village and neighbourhood. An IP address consists of a series of 32 binary bits (1s and 0s). It is very difficult for humans to read a binary IP address. For this reason, the 32 bits are grouped into four 8-bit bytes called octets. An IP address, even in this grouped format, is hard for humans to read, write, and remember. Therefore, each octet is presented as its decimal value, separated by a decimal point or period. This format is called dotted-decimal notation. When a host is configured with an IP address, it is entered as a dotted-decimal number, such as 192.168.1.5.

Imagine if you had to enter the 32-bit binary equivalent of this: 11000000101010000000000100000101. If you mistyped just 1 bit, the address would be different, and the host may not be able to communicate on the network. The logical 32-bit IP address is hierarchical and is composed of two parts. The first part identifies the network, and the second part identifies a host on that network. Both parts are required in an IP address. For example, if a host has an IP address of 192.168.18.57, the first three octets, 192.168.18, identify the network portion of the address, and the last octet, 57, identifies the host. This is called hierarchical addressing, because the network portion indicates the network on which each unique host address is located. Routers only need to know how to reach each network, not the location of each individual host. IP addresses are divided into the following five classes:

♦   **Class A** is for large networks, implemented by large companies and some countries.
♦   **Class B** is for medium-sized networks, implemented by universities.
♦   **Class C** is for small networks, implemented by ISPs for customer subscriptions.
♦   **Class D** is for special use for multicasting.
♦   **Class E** is used for experimental testing.

5.10   SUBNET MASK
The *subnet mask* indicates the network portion of an IP address. Like the IP address, the subnet mask is a dotted-decimal number. Usually all hosts within a LAN use the same subnet mask. Figure 5-8 shows default subnet masks for usable IP addresses that are mapped to the first three classes of IP addresses:

♦   **255.0.0.0:** Class A, which indicates that the first octet of the IP address is the network portion

♦   **255.255.0.0:** Class B, which indicates that the first two octets of the IP address are the network portion

♦   **255.255.255.0:**   Class C, which indicates that the first three octets of the IP address are the network portion.

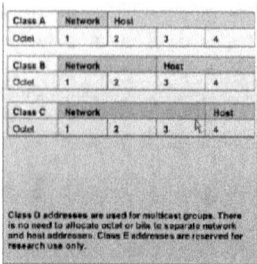

Figure 5.8 IP Address Classes

If an organization owns one Class B network but needs to provide IP addresses for four LANs, the organization would have to subdivide the Class B address into four smaller parts. Subnetting is a logical division of a network. It provides the means to divide a network, and the subnet mask specifies how it is subdivided. An experienced network administrator typically performs subnetting. After the subnetting scheme has been created, the proper IP addresses and subnet masks can be configured on the hosts in the four LANs. These skills are taught in the Cisco Networking Academy courses related to CCNA-level networking skills.

5.11 MANUAL CONFIGURATION

In a network with a small number of hosts, it is easy to manually configure each device with the proper IP address. A network administrator who understands IP addressing should assign the addresses and should know how to choose a valid address for a particular network. The IP address that is entered is unique for each host within the same network or subnet.

To manually enter an IP address on a host, go to the TCP/IP settings in the Properties window for the Network Interface Card (NIC). The NIC is the hardware that enables a computer to connect to a network. It has an address called the MAC address. Whereas the IP address is a logical address that is defined by the network administrator, a MAC address is "burned in," or permanently programmed into the NIC when it is manufactured. The IP address of a NIC can be changed, but the MAC address never changes. The main difference between an IP address and a MAC address is that the MAC address is used to deliver frames on the LAN, while an IP address is used to transport frames outside the LAN. A frame is a data packet, along with address information added to the beginning and end of the packet before transmission over the network. After a frame is delivered to the destination LAN, the MAC address is used to deliver the frame to the end host on that LAN. If more than a few computers comprise the LAN, manually configuring IP addresses for every host on the network can be time-consuming and prone to errors. In this case, using a Dynamic Host Configuration Protocol (DHCP) server would automatically assign IP addresses and greatly simplify the addressing process.

5.12 DYNAMIC OF HOST CONFIGURATION PROTOCOL (DHCP)

Dynamic Host Configuration Protocol (DHCP) is a software utility used to dynamically assign IP addresses to network devices. This dynamic process eliminates the need to manually assign IP addresses. A DHCP server can be set up and the hosts can be configured to automatically obtain an IP address. When a computer is set to obtain an IP address automatically, all the others IP addressing configuration boxes are dimmed, as shown in Figure 5.9. The server maintains a list of IP addresses to assign, and it manages the process so that every device on the network receives a unique IP address. Each address is held for a predetermined amount of time. When the time expires, the DHCP server can use this address for any computer that joins the network.

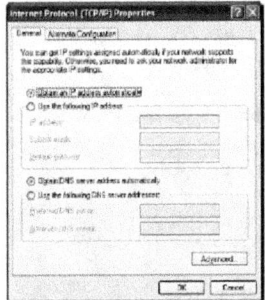

Figure 5.9 TCP/IP Properties

This is the IP address information that a DHCP server can assign to hosts:

♦   IP address

♦   Subnet mask

♦   Default gateway

♦   Optional values, such as a *Domain Name System (DNS) server* address

The DHCP server receives a request from a host. The server then selects IP address information from a set of predefined addresses that are stored in a database. After the IP address information is selected, the DHCP server offers these values to the requesting host on the network. If the host accepts the offer, the DHCP server leases the IP address for a specific period of time.

Using a DHCP server simplifies the administration of a network because the software keeps track of IP addresses. Automatically configuring TCP/IP also reduces the possibility of assigning duplicate or invalid IP addresses. Before a computer on the network can take advantage of the DHCP server services, the computer must be able to identify the server on the local network. You can configure a computer to accept an IP address from a DHCP server by clicking the **Obtain an IP address automatically** option in the NIC configuration window, as shown in Figure 5.9.

If your computer cannot communicate with the DHCP server to obtain an IP address, the Windows operating system automatically assigns a private IP address. If your computer is assigned an IP address in the range of 169.254.0.0 to 169.254.255.255, it can communicate with only other computers in the same range. An example of when these private addresses would be useful is in a classroom lab where you want to prevent access outside to your network.

This operating system feature is called Automatic Private IP Addressing (APIPA). APIPA continually requests an IP address from a DHCP server for your computer.

5.13   INTERNET PROTOCOLS AND APPLICATIONS

A protocol is a set of rules. Internet protocols are sets of rules governing communication within and between computers on a network. Protocol specifications define the format of the messages that are exchanged. A letter sent through the postal system also uses protocols. Part of the protocol specifies where on the envelope the delivery address needs to be written. If the delivery address is written in the wrong place, the letter cannot be delivered. Timing is crucial to network operation. Protocols require messages to arrive within a certain amount of time so that computers do not wait indefinitely for messages that may have been lost. Therefore, systems maintain one or more timers during transmission of data. Protocols also initiate alternative actions if the network does not meet the timing rules. Many protocols consist of a suite of other protocols that are stacked in layers. These layers depend on the operation of the other layers in the suite to function properly.

These are the main functions of protocols:
♦   Identifying errors
♦   Compressing the data
♦   Deciding how the data is to be sent
♦   Addressing the data
♦   Deciding how to announce sent and received data

Although many other protocols exist, Table 5.9 summarizes the functions of some of the more common protocols used on networks and the Internet.
To understand how networks and the Internet work, you must be familiar with the commonly used protocols. These protocols are used to browse the web, send and receive e-mail, and transfer data files. You will encounter other protocols as your experience in IT grows, but they are not used as often as the common protocols described here:

♦   **TCP/IP**: The TCP/IP suite of protocols has become the dominant standard for internetworking.
TCP/IP represents a set of public standards that specify how packets of information are exchanged between computers over one or more networks.

♦   **IPX/SPX**: Internetwork Packet Exchange/Sequenced Packet Exchange is the protocol suite originally employed by Novell Corporation's network operating system, NetWare. It delivers functions similar to those included in TCP/IP. Novell in its current releases supports the TCP/IP suite. A large installed base of NetWare networks continue to use IPX/SPX.

♦   **NetBEUI**: NetBIOS Extended User Interface is a protocol used primarily on small Windows NT networks. NetBEUI cannot be routed or used by routers to talk to each other on a large network. NetBEUI is suitable for small peer-to-peer networks, involving a few computers directly connected to each other. It can be used in conjunction with another routable protocol such as

TCP/IP. This gives the network administrator the advantages of the high performance of NetBEUI within the local network and the ability to communicate beyond the LAN over TCP/IP.

♦   **AppleTalk:** AppleTalk is a protocol suite to network Macintosh computers. It is composed of a comprehensive set of protocols that span the seven layers of the Open Systems Interconnection (OSI) reference model. The AppleTalk protocol was designed to run over LocalTalk, which is the Apple LAN physical topology. This protocol is also designed to run over major LAN types, notably Ethernet and Token Ring.

♦   *HTTP*: Hypertext Transfer Protocol governs how files such as text, graphics, sound, and video are exchanged on the World Wide Web (WWW). The Internet Engineering Task Force (IETF) developed the standards for HTTP.

♦   *FTP*: File Transfer Protocol provides services for file transfer and manipulation. FTP allows multiple simultaneous connections to remote file systems.

Protocols Function

♦   **SSH:** Secure Shell is used to securely connect to a remote computer.

♦   *Telnet*: An application used to connect to a remote computer that lacks security features.

♦   **POP3:** Post Office Protocol is used to download e-mail from a remote mail server.

♦   **IMAP:** Internet Message Access Protocol is also used to download e-mail from a remote mail server.

♦   *SMTP*: Simple Mail Transfer Protocol is used to send e-mail to a remote e-mail server. The more you understand about each of these protocols, the more you will understand how networks and the Internet work.

Define ICMP

Devices on a network use *Internet Control Message Protocol (ICMP)* to send control and error messages to computers and servers. ICMP has several different uses, such as announcing network errors, announcing network congestion, and troubleshooting. Packet Internet groper (ping) is commonly used to test connections between computers. Ping is a simple but highly useful command-line utility that determines whether a specific IP address is accessible. You can ping the IP address to test IP connectivity. Ping works by sending an ICMP echo request to a destination computer or other network device. The receiving device then sends back an ICMP echo reply message to confirm connectivity. Ping is a troubleshooting tool used to determine basic connectivity. Example 8-1 shows the command-line switches that can be used with the **ping** command. Four ICMP echo requests (pings) are sent to the destination computer. If it can be reached, the destination computer responds with four ICMP echo replies. The percentage of successful replies can help you determine the reliability and accessibility of the destination computer.

5.14 THE PHYSICAL COMPONENTS OF A NETWORK

Many devices can be used in a network to provide connectivity, as shown in Figure 5.10.

Which device you use depends on how many devices you are connecting, the type of connections they use, and the speed at which the devices operate. These are the most common devices on a network:

♦   Computers

♦   Hubs

♦   Switches

♦   Routers

♦   Wireless access points

Figure 5.10 Physical Network Components

The physical components of a network are needed to move data between these devices. The characteristics of the media determine where and how the components are used. These are the most common media used on networks:

♦   Twisted pair

♦   Fiber-optic cabling

♦   Radio waves

After completing this section, you will meet these objectives:

♦   Identify the names, purposes, and characteristics of network devices.

♦   Identify the names, purposes, and characteristics of common network cables.

5.15 CHARACTERISTICS OF NETWORK DEVICES

To make data transmission more extensible and efficient than a simple peer-to-peer network, network designers use specialized network devices such as hubs, switches, routers, and wireless access points to send data between devices.

Hubs

Hubs, shown in Figure 5.11, are devices that extend a network's range by receiving data on one port and then regenerating the data and sending it out to all other ports. This process means that all traffic from a device connected to the hub is sent to all the other devices connected to the hub every time the hub transmits data. This causes a large amount of network traffic. Hubs are also called concentrators because they serve as a central connection point for a LAN. They are also sometimes called multiport repeaters because they send data out all the ports.

Figure 5.11 Hub

Bridges and Switches

Files are broken into small pieces of data, called packets, before they are transmitted over a network. This process allows for error checking and easier retransmission if the packet is lost or corrupted. Address information is added to the beginning and end of packets before they are transmitted. The packet, along with the address information, is called a frame.

LANs are often divided into sections called segments, similar to how a company is divided into departments. The boundaries of segments can be defined using a bridge. A *bridge* is a device used to filter network traffic between LAN segments. Bridges keep a record of all the devices on each segment to which the bridge is connected. When the bridge receives a frame, it examines the destination address to determine if the frame is to be sent to a different segment, or dropped. The bridge also helps improve the flow of data by keeping frames confined to only the segment to which the frame belongs.

Switches, shown in Figure 5.12, are sometimes called multiport bridges. A typical bridge may have just two ports, linking two segments of the same network. A switch has several ports, depending on how many network segments are to be linked. A switch is a more sophisticated device than a bridge. A switch maintains a table of the MAC addresses for computers that are connected to each port. When a frame arrives at a port, the switch compares the address information in the frame to its MAC address table. The switch then determines which port to use to forward the frame.

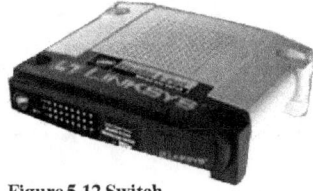

Figure 5.12 Switch

5.16 ROUTERS

Whereas a switch connects segments of a network, *routers*, shown in Figure 5.13, are devices that connect entire networks to each other. Switches use MAC addresses to forward a frame within a single network. Routers use IP addresses to forward frames to other networks. A router can be a computer with special network software installed, or it can be a device built by network equipment manufacturers. Routers contain tables of IP addresses along with optimal destination routes to other networks.

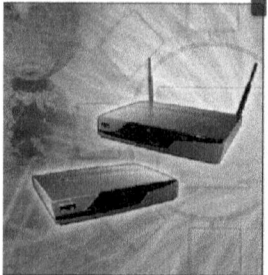

Figure 5.13 Routers

5.17 WIRELESS ACCESS POINTS

Wireless access points, shown in Figure 5.14, provide network access to wireless devices such as laptops and PDAs. The wireless access point uses radio waves to communicate with radios in computers, PDAs, and other wireless access points. An access point has a limited range of coverage. Large networks require several access points to provide adequate wireless coverage.

Figure 5.14 Wireless Access Point
Multipurpose Devices

Some network devices perform more than one function. It is more convenient to purchase and configure one device that serves all your needs than to purchase a separate device for each function. This is especially true for the home user. In your home, you would purchase a multipurpose device instead of a switch, a router, and a wireless access point. The Linksys 300N, shown in Figure 5.15, is an example of a multipurpose device.

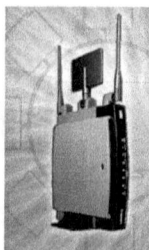

Figure 5.15 Multipurpose Device

Identification of Network Cables

Until recently, cables were the only medium used to connect devices on networks. A wide variety of networking cables are available. Coaxial and twisted-pair cables use copper to transmit data. Fiber-optic cables use glass or plastic to transmit data. These cables differ in bandwidth, size, and cost. You need to know what type of cable to use in different situations so that you install the correct cables for the job. You also need to be able to troubleshoot and repair problems you encounter.

Twisted Pair

Twisted pair is a type of copper cabling that is used for telephone communications and most Ethernet networks. A pair of wires forms a circuit that can transmit data. The pair is twisted to provide protection against crosstalk, which is the noise generated by adjacent pairs of wires in the cable. Pairs of copper wires are encased in colour-coded plastic insulation and are twisted together. An outer jacket protects the bundles of twisted pairs. Figure 5-16 shows a twisted-pair cable.

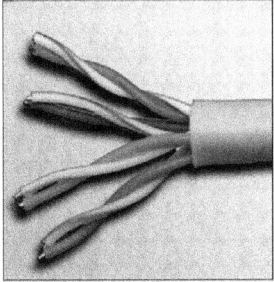

Figure 5.16 Twisted-Pair Cabling

When electricity flows through a copper wire, a magnetic field is created around the wire. A circuit has two wires, and in a circuit, the two wires have oppositely-charged magnetic fields. When the two wires of the circuit are next to each other, the magnetic fields cancel each other out. This is called the cancellation effect. Without the cancellation effect, your network communications become slow because of the interference caused by the magnetic fields.

The two basic types of twisted-pair cables are as follows:

♦   *Unshielded twisted pair (UTP)* is cable that has two or four pairs of wires. This type of cable relies solely on the cancellation effect produced by the twisted-wire pairs that limits signal degradation caused by electromagnetic interface (EMI) and radio frequency interference (RFI). UTP is the most commonly used cabling in networks. UTP cables have a range of 328 feet (100 m).

♦   With *shielded twisted pair (STP)*, each pair of wires is wrapped in metallic foil to better shield the wires from noise. Four pairs of wires are then wrapped in an overall metallic braid or foil. STP reduces electrical noise from within the cable. It also reduces EMI and RFI from outside the cable.

Although STP prevents interference better than UTP, STP is more expensive because of extra shielding. It also is more difficult to install because of the thickness. In addition, the metallic shielding must be grounded at both ends. If it's improperly grounded, the shield acts like an antenna, picking up unwanted signals. STP is primarily used outside North America. STP cables also have a range of 328 feet (100 m).

Category Rating
UTP comes in several categories that are based on two factors:
♦   The number of wires in the cable
♦   The number of twists in those wires
Category 3 is the wiring used for telephone systems and Ethernet LAN at 10 Mbps. Category 3 has four pairs of wires.

Category 5 and Category 5e have four pairs of wires with a transmission rate of 100 Mbps. Category 5 and Category 5e are the most common network cables used. Category 5e has more twists per foot than Category 5 wiring. These extra twists further prevent interference from outside sources and the other wires within the cable.

Some Category 6 cables use a plastic divider to separate the pairs of wires, which prevents interference. The pairs also have more twists than Category 5e cable.

5.18   COAXIAL CABLE

Coaxial cable is a copper-cored cable surrounded by a heavy shielding, as shown in Figure 5.17.

Coaxial cable is used to connect the computers to the rest of the network. Coaxial cable uses BNC connectors, sometimes called "British Naval Connectors" or "Bayonet Neill-Concelman" connectors, at the ends of the cables to make the connection. Several types of coaxial cable exist:

♦   *Thicknet (10BASE5)* is coaxial cable that was used in networks and operated at 10Mbps, with a maximum length of 500 meters.

♦   *Thinnet (10BASE2)* is coaxial cable that was used in networks and operated at 10Mbps, with a maximum length of 185 meters.

♦   **RG-59** is most commonly used for cable television in the U.S.

♦   **RG-6** is higher-quality cable than RG-59, with more bandwidth and less susceptibility to interference.

Fiber-Optic Cable
An optical fiber is a glass or plastic conductor that transmits information using light. *Fiberoptic cable*, shown in Figure 8-18, has one or more optical fibers enclosed in a sheath or jacket. Because it is made of glass, fiber-optic cable is not affected by EMI or RFI. All signals are converted to light pulses to enter the cable and are converted back into electrical signals when they leave it. This means that fiber-optic cable can deliver signals that are clearer, that can go farther, and that have greater bandwidth than cable made of copper or other metals.

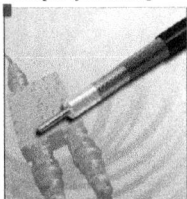

Figure 5.17 Coaxial Cabling

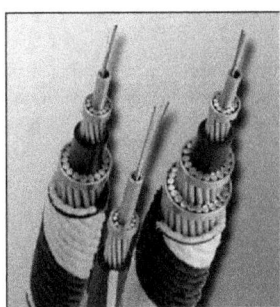

Figure 5.18 Fiber-Optic Cabling

Fiber-optic cable can reach distances of several miles or kilometers before the signal needs to be regenerated. Fiber-optic cable usually is more expensive to use than copper cable, and the connectors are more costly and harder to assemble. Common connectors for fiber-optic networks are SC, ST, and LC. These three types of fiber-optic connectors are half-duplex, which allows data to flow in only one direction. Therefore, two cables are needed.

These are the two types of glass fiber-optic cable:

♦   *Multimode* is cable that has a thicker core than single-mode cable. It is easier to make, can use simpler light sources (LEDs), and works well over distances of a few kilometres or less.

♦   *Single-mode* is cable that has a very thin core. It is harder to make, uses lasers as a light source, and can transmit signals dozens of kilometers with ease. A fiber-optic cable is one or more optical fibers enclosed together in a sheath or jacket.

5.19   LAN TOPOLOGIES AND ARCHITECTURES

Most of the computers that you work on will be part of a network. Topologies and architectures are building blocks for designing a computer network. Although you may not build a computer network, you need to understand how they are designed so that you can work on computers that are part of a network. The two types of LAN topologies are physical and logical. A physical topology, shown in Figure 5.19, is the physical layout of the components on the network. A *logical topology*, shown in Figure 5-20, determines how the hosts communicate across a medium, such as a cable or the airwaves. Topologies commonly are represented as network diagrams.

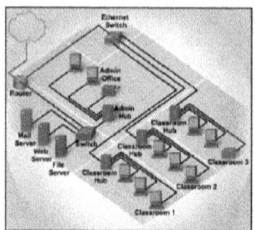

Figure 5.19 Physical Topology

A LAN architecture is built around a topology. A LAN architecture comprises all the components that make up the structure of a communications system. These components include the hardware, software, protocols, and sequence of operations. After completing this section, you will meet these objectives:

◆   Describe LAN architectures.
◆   Describe LAN topologies.

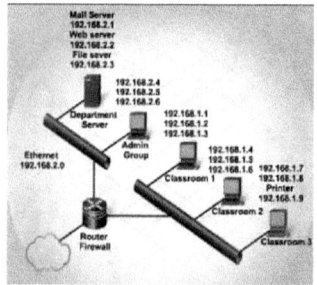

Figure 5.20 Logical Topology

LAN Architectures
A LAN architecture describes both the physical and logical topologies used in a network.

Table 5-1 lists the three most common LAN architectures.
Table 5-1 LAN Architectures

Architecture	Physical Topology	Logical Topology
Ethernet	Bus	Star
Extended star	Bus	
Token Ring	Star	Ring
Fiber Distributed Data Interface (FDDI)	Double ring	Ethernet.

The *Ethernet* architecture is based on the IEEE 802.3 standard. The IEEE 802.3 standard specifies that a network must use the carrier sense multiple access collision detect (CSMA/CD) access control method. In CSMA/CD, hosts access the network using the first come, first-served broadcast topology method to transmit data. Ethernet uses a logical bus or broadcast topology and either a bus or star physical topology. As networks expand, most Ethernet networks are implemented using an extended star or hierarchical star topology. Standard transfer rates are 10 Mbps and 100 Mbps, but new standards outline Gigabit Ethernet, which can attain speeds of up to 1000 Mbps (1 Gbps).

LAN Topologies

A physical topology defines the way in which computers, printers, and other devices are connected to a network. A logical topology describes how the hosts access the medium and communicates on the network. The type of topology, as shown in Figure 5-21, determines the network's capabilities, such as ease of setup, speed, and cable lengths.

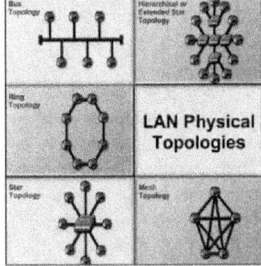

Figure 5.21 LAN Physical Topologies

Physical Topologies

The common LAN physical topologies are as follows:

♦   ***Bus Topology***: In the bus topology, each computer connects to a common cable. The cable connects one computer to the next, like a bus line going through a city. The cable has a small cap installed at the end, called a terminator. The terminator prevents signals from bouncing back and causing network errors.

♦   ***Ring Topology***: In a ring topology, hosts are connected in a physical ring or circle. Because the ring topology has no beginning or end, the cable does not need to be terminated. A specially formatted frame, called a token, travels around the ring, stopping at each host. If a host wants to transmit data, it adds the data and the destination address to the frame. The frame then continues around the ring until it stops at the host with the destination address. The destination host takes the data out of the frame.

♦   ***Star Topology***: The star topology has a central connection point, which normally is a device such as a hub, switch, or router. Each host on a network has a cable segment that attaches the host directly to the central connection point. The advantage of a star topology is that it is easy to troubleshoot. Each host is connected to the central device with its own wire. If there is a problem with that cable, only that host is affected. The rest of the network remains operational.

♦   ***Hierarchical or Extended Star Topology***: A hierarchical or extended star topology is a star network with an additional networking device connected to the main networking device. Typically, a network cable connects to one hub, and then several other hubs connect to the first hub. Larger networks, such as those of corporations or universities, use the hierarchical star topology.

♦   *Mesh Topology*: The mesh topology connects all devices to each other. When every device is connected to every other device, a failure of any cable does not affect the network. The mesh topology is used in WANs that interconnect LANs. Logical Topologies, the two most common types of logical topologies are broadcast and token passing. In a broadcast topology, each host addresses data to either a particular host or to all hosts connected on a network. There is no order that the hosts must follow to use the network. It is first come, first served for transmitting data on the network. Token passing controls network access by passing an electronic token sequentially to each host. When a host receives the token, it can send data on the network. If the host has no data to send, it passes the token to the next host, and the process repeats.

Token Ring
IBM originally developed *Token Ring* as a reliable network architecture based on the token-passing access control method. Token Ring is used with computers and mainframes. Token Ring is an example of an architecture in which the physical topology is different from its logical topology. The Token Ring topology is called a star-wired ring because the outer appearance of the network design is a star. The computers connect to a central hub, called a multistation access unit (MSAU). Inside the device, however, the wiring forms a circular data path, creating a logical ring. The logical ring is created by the token travelling out of an MSAU port to a computer. If the computer does not have any data to send, the token is sent back to the MSAU port and then out the next port to the next computer. This process continues for all computers and therefore resembles a physical ring.

FDDI
FDDI is a type of Token Ring network. The implementation and topology of FDDI differs from the IBM Token Ring LAN architecture. FDDI is often used to connect several buildings in an office complex or on a university campus. FDDI runs on fiber-optic cable. FDDI combines high-speed performance with the advantages of the token-passing ring topology. FDDI runs at 100 Mbps on a dual-ring topology. The outer ring is called the primary ring, and the inner ring is called the secondary ring. Normally, traffic flows on only the primary ring. If the primary ring fails, the data automatically flows onto the secondary ring in the opposite direction.

An FDDI dual ring supports a maximum of 500 computers per ring. The total distance of each length of the cable ring is 62 miles (100 km). A repeater, which is a device that regenerates signals, is required every 1.2 miles (2 km). In recent years, many Token Ring networks have been replaced by faster Ethernet networks.

5.20   STANDARDS ORGANIZATIONS
Several worldwide standards organizations are responsible for setting networking standards. Manufacturers use standards as a basis for developing technology, especially communications and networking technologies. Standardizing technology ensures that the devices you use are compatible with other devices using the same technology. Standards groups create, examine, and update standards. These standards are applied to the development of technology to meet the demands for higher bandwidth, efficient communication, and reliable service.

Here is a list of standards organizations:

♦ **IEEE:** The Institute of Electrical and Electronic Engineers is a nonprofit technical professional association of more than 377,000 members in 150 countries. Founded in 1884, the organization is composed of engineers, scientists, and students. Through its members, the IEEE is a leading authority in technical areas ranging from computer engineering, biomedical technology, and telecommunications to electric power, aerospace, and consumer electronics.

♦ **ISO:** The International Organization for Standardization is an international organization composed of national standards bodies from more than 140 countries. The American National Standards Institute (ANSI), for example, is a member of ISO. ISO is a nongovernment organization established to promote the development of standardization and related activities. ISO's work results in international agreements, which are published as International Standards.

ISO has defined a number of important computer standards, the most significant of which is perhaps the OSI model, a standardized architecture for designing networks.

ISO together with the International Electrotechnical Commission (IEC) and the International Telecommunication Union (ITU) have built a strategic partnership with the World Trade Organization (WTO).

♦ **IAB:** The Internet Architecture Board is the committee that oversees the technical and engineering development of the Internet by the Internet Society (ISOC). The committee oversees the Internet Engineering Task Force (IETF) and the Internet Research Task Force (IRTF). When the Internet transitioned to a public entity in 1992, the name was changed to what it is today, the Internet Architecture Board, originally formed by the U.S. Department of Defense.

♦ **IEC:** Founded in 1906, the International Electrotechnical Commission is the global organization that prepares and publishes international standards for all electrical, electronic, and related technologies. The IEC was founded because of a resolution passed at the International Electrical Congress held in St. Louis (U.S.) in 1904. The membership consists of more than 60 participating countries, including all the world's major trading nations and a growing number of industrialized countries. The IEC's mission is to promote, through its members, international cooperation on all questions related to electrotechnologies, electroacoustics, multimedia, telecommunications, and energy production and distribution, as well as associated general disciplines such as terminology and symbols, electromagnetic compatibility, design and development, safety, and the environment.

The IEC is one of the bodies recognized by the World Trade Organization (WTO) and entrusted by it to monitor the national and regional organizations agreeing to use the IEC's international standards as the basis of national or regional standards as part of the WTO's Technical Barriers to Trade Agreement.

♦ **ANSI:** The American National Standards Institute is a private, nonprofit organization that administers and coordinates the U.S. voluntary standardization and conformity assessment system. ANSI identifies industrial and public requirements for national consensus standards and coordinates and manages their development, resolves national standards problems, and ensures effective participation in international standardization.

Since 1918, the institute's mission has been to enhance both the global competitiveness of U.S. business and quality of life by promoting and facilitating voluntary consensus standards and conformity assessment systems and safeguarding their integrity. ANSI does not develop standards itself. Rather, it facilitates development by establishing consensus processes among qualified groups. This is why its acronym is seen on many standards.

♦   **TIA/EIA:** The Telecommunications Industry Association (TIA) and Electronic Industries Association (EIA) are trade associations that jointly develop and publish a series of standards covering structured voice and data wiring for LANs. These industry standards evolved after the U.S. telephone industry deregulation in 1984, which transferred responsibility for on-premises cabling to the building owner. Before that, AT&T used proprietary cables and systems.

Ethernet Standards
Ethernet protocols describe the rules that control how communication occurs on an Ethernet network. To ensure that all Ethernet devices are compatible with each other, the IEEE developed standards for manufacturers and programmers to follow when developing Ethernet devices. Figure 8.22 shows an example of how different devices can communicate using these standards.

Figure 8.22 Interoperability Between Standards

After completing this section, you will meet these objectives:
♦   Explain cabled Ethernet standards.
♦   Explain wireless Ethernet standards.

Cabled Ethernet Standards
The Ethernet architecture is based on the IEEE 802.3 standard. The *IEEE 802.3* standard specifies that a network must implement the CSMA/CD access control method. In *CSMA/CD*, all end stations "listen" to the network wire for clearance to send data. This process is similar to waiting to hear a dial tone on a phone before dialing a number. When the end station detects that no other host is transmitting, it attempts to send data. If no other station sends data at the same time, the transmission arrives at the destination computer with no problems. If another end station observes the same clear signal and transmits at the same time, a collision occurs on the network medium.

The first station that detects the collision, or the doubling of voltage, sends out a jam signal that tells all stations to stop transmitting and to run a backoff algorithm. A backoff algorithm calculates random times at which the end station retries the network transmission. This random time typically is one or two milliseconds (ms), or thousandths of a second.

This sequence occurs every time a collision occurs on the network and can reduce Ethernet transmission by up to 40 percent. Ethernet Technologies The IEEE 802.3 standard defines several physical implementations that support Ethernet. Some of the common implementations are described here.

Ethernet **10BASE-T** is an Ethernet technology that uses a star topology. 10BASE-T is a popular Ethernet architecture whose features are indicated in its name:

♦ The 10 represents a speed of 10 Mbps.

♦ BASE represents baseband transmission. In baseband transmission, the entire bandwidth of a cable is used for one type of signal.

♦ The T represents twisted-pair copper cabling.

The advantages of 10BASE-T are as follows:

♦ Installation of cable is inexpensive compared to fiber-optic installation.

♦ Cables are thin, flexible, and easier to install than coaxial cabling.

♦ Equipment and cables are easy to upgrade.

The disadvantages of 10BASE-T are as follows:

♦ The maximum length of a 10BASE-T segment is only 328 feet (100 m).

♦ Cables are susceptible to EMI.

Fast Ethernet

The high-bandwidth demands of many modern applications, such as videoconferencing and streaming audio, have created a need for higher data-transfer speeds. Many networks require more bandwidth than 10 Mbps Ethernet. 100BASE-TX is much faster than 10BASE-T and has a theoretical bandwidth of 100 Mbps.

The advantages of 100BASE-TX are as follows:

♦ At 100 Mbps, transfer rates of 100BASE-TX are ten times that of 10BASE-T.

♦ 100BASE-X uses twisted-pair cabling, which is inexpensive and easy to install.

The disadvantages of 100BASE-TX are as follows:

♦ The maximum length of a 100BASE-TX segment is only 328 feet (100 m).

♦ Cables are susceptible to EMI.

Gigabit Ethernet 1000BASE-T is commonly known as Gigabit Ethernet. Gigabit Ethernet is a LAN architecture. The advantages of 1000BASE-T are as follows:

♦ The 1000BASE-T architecture supports data transfer rates of 1 Gbps. At 1 Gbps, it is ten times faster than Fast Ethernet and 100 times faster than Ethernet. This increased speed makes it possible to implement bandwidth-intensive applications, such as live video.

♦ The 1000BASE-T architecture is interoperable with 10BASE-T and 100BASE-TX. The disadvantages of 1000BASE-T are as follows:

♦ The maximum length of a 1000BASE-T segment is only 328 feet (100 m).
♦ It is susceptible to interference.
♦ Gigabit NICs and switches are expensive.
♦ Additional equipment is required.

Wireless Ethernet Standards

IEEE 802.11 is the standard that specifies connectivity for wireless networks. IEEE 802.11, or Wi-Fi, refers to the collective group of standards802.11a, 802.11b, 802.11g, and 802.11n. These protocols specify the frequencies, speeds, and other capabilities of the different Wi-Fi standards:

♦ ***802.11a***: Devices conforming to the 802.11a standard allow WLANs to achieve data rates as high as 54 Mbps. IEEE 802.11a devices operate in the 5-GHz radio frequency range and within a maximum range of 150 feet (45.7 m).

♦ ***802.11b***: 802.11b operates in the 2.4-GHz frequency range, with a maximum theoretical data rate of 11 Mbps. These devices operate within a maximum range of 300 feet (91 m).

♦ ***802.11g***: IEEE 802.11g provides the same theoretical maximum speed as 802.11a, which is 54 Mbps, but operates in the same 2.4-GHz spectrum as 802.11b. Unlike 802.11a, 802.11g is backward-compatible with 802.11b. 802.11g also has a maximum range of 300 feet (91 m).

♦ ***802.11n***: 802.11n is a newer wireless standard that has a theoretical bandwidth of 540 Mbps and operates in either the 2.4-GHz or 5-GHz frequency range with a maximum range of 984 feet (250 m).

5.21   THE OSI AND TCP/IP DATA MODELS

An architectural model is a common frame of reference for explaining Internet communications and developing communication protocols. It separates the functions of protocols into manageable layers. Each layer performs a specific function in the process of communicating over a network.

The TCP/IP model was created by researchers in the U.S. Department of Defense (DoD). The TCP/IP model is a tool used to help explain the TCP/IP suite of protocols, which is the dominant standard for transporting data across networks. This model has four layers, as In the early 1980s, the ISO developed the Open Systems Interconnection (OSI) model, which was defined in ISO standard 7498-1, to standardize how devices communicate on a network. This model has seven layers, as shown in Table 5.5. This model was a major step toward ensuring that network devices could interoperate. After completing this section, you will meet these objectives:

♦ Define the TCP/IP model.
♦ Define the OSI model.
♦ Compare the OSI and TCP/IP models.

Define the TCP/IP Model

The TCP/IP reference model provides a common frame of reference for developing the protocols used on the Internet. It consists of layers that perform functions necessary to prepare data for transmission over a network. Table 8-6 describes the four layers of the TCP/IP model.

A message begins at the top layer, the application layer, and moves down the TCP/IP layers to the bottom layer, the network access layer. Header information is added to the message as it moves down through each layer and then is transmitted. After reaching the destination, the message travels back up through each layer of the TCP/IP model. The header information that was added to the message is stripped away as the message moves up through the layers toward its destination.

Application Protocols

Application layer protocols provide network services to user applications such as web browsers and e-mail programs. Here are some of the *application protocols* that operate at the TCP/IP application layer:

♦   **Hypertext Transfer Protocol (HTTP)** governs how files such as text, graphics, sound, and video are exchanged on the Internet or World Wide Web (WWW). HTTP is an application layer protocol. A web server runs an HTTP service or daemon. A daemon is a program that services HTTP requests. These requests are transmitted by HTTP client software, which is another name for a web browser.

♦   **Telnet** is an application that you can use to access, control, and troubleshoot remote computers and network devices.

♦   **File Transfer Protocol (FTP)** is a set of rules governing how files are transferred. FTP allows multiple simultaneous connections to remote file systems.

♦   **Simple Mail Transport Protocol (SMTP)** provides messaging services over TCP/IP and supports most Internet e-mail programs.

♦   *Domain Name System (DNS)* translates domain names, such as www.cisco.com, to IP addresses.

♦   *Hypertext Markup Language (HTML)* is a page description language. Web designers use HTML to indicate to web browser software how the page should look. HTML includes tags to indicate boldface and italic type, line breaks, paragraph breaks, hyperlinks, and insertion of tables, among other instructions.

5.22   TRANSPORT PROTOCOLS

Transport layer protocols provide end-to-end management of the data. One of the functions of these protocols is to divide the data into manageable segments for easier transport across the network. Here are the two *transport protocols* that operate at the TCP/IP transport layer:

♦   *Transmission Control Protocol (TCP)* is the primary Internet protocol for the reliable delivery of data. TCP includes facilities for end-to-end connection establishment, error detection and recovery, and metering the rate of data flow into the network. Many standard applications, such as e-mail, web browser, file transfer, and Telnet, depend on the services of TCP.

♦   *User Datagram Protocol (UDP)* offers a connectionless service for delivery of data. UDP uses lower overhead than TCP and doesn't handle issues of reliability. Network management applications, network file system, and simple file transport use UDP. Internet Protocols Internet layer protocols operate at the third layer from the top in the TCP/IP model. Internet protocols are used to provide connectivity between hosts in the network. Here are some of the protocols that operate at the TCP/IP Internet layer:

♦   ***Internet Protocol (IP)*** provides source and destination addressing, much like the address and return address on a postal envelope. In conjunction with routing protocols, IP provides packet-forwarding information from one network to another.

♦   **Internet Control Message Protocol (ICMP)** is used for network testing and troubleshooting. It enables diagnostic and error messages. The ping application uses ICMP echo messages to test if a remote device can be reached.

♦   ***Routing Information Protocol (RIP)*** operates between router devices to discover paths between networks. In an intranet, routers depend on a routing protocol to build and maintain information about how to forward packets toward the destination. RIP chooses routes based on the distance or hop count to the destination.

♦   ***Address Resolution Protocol (ARP)*** is used to map the MAC address of a node on the network when its IP address is known. End stations as well as routers use ARP to discover MAC addresses.

Network Access Protocols
Network access protocols describe the standards that hosts use to access the physical media. The IEEE 802.3 Ethernet standards and technologies, such as CSMA/CD and 10BASE-T, are defined at this layer.

Define the OSI Model
The OSI model is an industry-standard framework that is used to divide network communications into seven distinct layers. Although other models exist, most network vendors today build their products using this framework.

A system that implements protocol behavior consisting of a series of these layers is known as a protocol stack. Protocol stacks can be implemented in either hardware or software, or a combination of both. Typically, only the lower layers are implemented in hardware, and the higher layers are implemented in software

When data is transferred, it is said to virtually travel down the OSI model layers of the sending computer and up the OSI model layers of the receiving computer. When a user wants to send data, such as an e-mail, the encapsulation process starts at the application layer. The application layer provides network access to applications Information flows through the top three layers and is considered to be data when it gets down to the transport layer. At the transport layer, the data is broken into more manageable segments, or transport layer protocol data units (PDU), for orderly transport across the network. A PDU describes data as it moves from one layer of the OSI model to another. The transport layer PDU also contains information such as port numbers, sequence numbers, and acknowledgment numbers, which is used for reliable data transport.

At the network layer, each segment from the transport layer becomes a packet. The packet contains logical addressing and other Layer 3 control information. At the data link layer, each packet from the network layer becomes a frame. The frame contains physical address and error-correction information. At the physical layer, the frame becomes bits. These bits are transmitted one at a time across the network medium.

At the receiving computer, the de-encapsulation process reverses the process of encapsulation. The bits arrive at the physical layer of the OSI model of the receiving computer. The process of virtually traveling up the OSI model of the receiving computer brings the data to the application layer, where an e-mail program displays the e-mail.

Note
Mnemonics can help you remember the seven layers of the OSI. Two examples are "All People Seem to Need Data Processing" and "Please Do Not Throw Sausage Pizza Away."

Compare the OSI and TCP/IP Models
The OSI model and the TCP/IP model are both reference models used to describe the data communication process. The TCP/IP model is used specifically for the TCP/IP suite of protocols.

The OSI model is used to develop standard communication for equipment and applications from different vendors.

The TCP/IP model performs the same process as the OSI model, but it uses four layers instead of seven. Figure 8.23 shows how the layers of the two models compare.

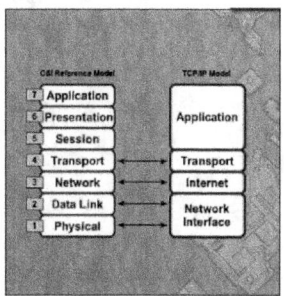

Figure 5.23 OSI Model and TCP/IP Model Compared

Describe How to Configure a NIC and a Modem
A network interface card (NIC) is required to connect to the Internet. The NIC may come preinstalled, or you may have to purchase one. In rare cases, you may need to update the *NIC driver*. You can use the driver disc that comes with the motherboard or adapter card, or you can supply a driver that you downloaded from the manufacturer. After the NIC and the driver have been installed, you can connect the computer to the network.

In addition to installing a NIC, you may need to install a modem to connect to the Internet. After completing this section, you will meet these objectives:

♦   Install or update a NIC driver.

♦   Attach the computer to an existing network.

♦   Describe the installation of a modem.

Install or Update a NIC Driver

Sometimes a manufacturer publishes new driver software for a NIC. A new driver may enhance the functionality of the NIC, or it may be needed for operating system compatibility. When installing a new driver, be sure to disable virus protection software so that none of the files is incorrectly installed. Some virus scanners detect a driver update as a possible virus attack. Also, only one driver should be installed at a time; otherwise, some updating processes may conflict.

A best practice is to close all applications that are running so that they do not use any files associated with the driver update. Before updating a driver, you should visit the manufacturer's website. In many cases, you can download a self-extracting executable driver file that automatically installs or updates the driver. Alternatively, you can click the Update Driver button in the Device Manager toolbar.

The + next to the Network adapters category allows you to expand the category and show the network adapters installed in your system. To view and change the adapter's properties, or update the driver, double-click the adapter. In the adapter properties window, click the Driver tab. Figure 8.24 shows an example of a network card adapter properties page in Device Manager. When the update is complete, it is a good idea to reboot the computer, even if you do not receive a message telling you to do so. Rebooting the computer ensures that the installation has gone as planned and that the new driver is working properly. When installing multiple drivers, reboot the computer between each update to make sure that no conflicts exist. This step takes extra time but ensures a clean installation of the driver.

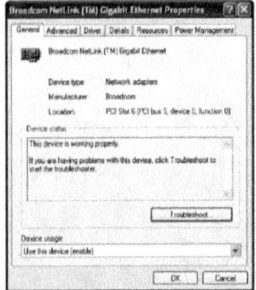

Figure 5.24 Adapter Properties in Device Manager

Uninstall a NIC Driver

If a new NIC driver does not perform as expected after it has been installed, the driver can be uninstalled, or rolled back, to the previous driver. Double-click the adapter in the Device Manager.

In the Adapter Properties window, click the Driver tab, and click Roll Back Driver. If no driver was installed before the update, this option is unavailable. In that case, you need to find a driver for the device and install it manually if the operating system cannot find a suitable driver for the NIC.

Attach the Computer to an Existing Network

Now that the NIC drivers are installed, you are ready to connect to the network. Plug a network cable, also called an Ethernet patch or straight-through cable, into the network port on the computer. Plug the other end into the network device or wall jack. After connecting the network cable, look at the LEDs, or link lights, next to the Ethernet port on the NIC to see if any activity is occurring. If no activity is going on, this may indicate a faulty cable, a faulty hub port, or even a faulty NIC. You may have to replace one or more of these devices to correct the problem.

After you have confirmed that the computer is connected to the network and that the link lights on the NIC indicate a working connection, the computer needs an IP address. Most networks are set up so that the computer receives an IP address automatically from a local DHCP server. If the computer does not have an IP address, you need to enter a unique IP address in the TCP/IP properties of the NIC.

Every NIC must be configured with the following information:

♦　**Protocols:** The same protocol must be implemented between any two computers that communicate on the same network.

♦　**IP address:** This address can be configured and must be unique to each device. The IP address can be manually configured or automatically assigned by DHCP.

♦　***MAC address*:** Each device has a unique MAC address. The MAC address is assigned by the manufacturer and cannot be changed.

After the computer is connected to the network, you should test connectivity with the **ping** command. Use the **ipconfig** command to find out what your IP address is. Example 5.3 shows sample output from the **ipconfig /all** command.

Ping your own IP address to make sure that your NIC is working properly. After you have determined that your NIC is working, **ping** your default gateway or another computer on your network, as shown in Example 5.4. A ***default gateway*** allows a host to communicate outside your network. If you have an Internet connection, ping a popular website, such as www.cisco.com. If you can successfully ping an Internet site or another computer on your network, everything is working properly with your connection. If you cannot ping one of these, you need to troubleshoot the connection.

5.23　INSTALLATION OF A MODEM

A modem, shown in Figure 5.25, is an electronic device that transfers data between one computer and another using analog signals over a telephone line. The modem converts digital data to analog signals for transmission. The modem at the receiving end reconverts the analog signals to digital data to be interpreted by the computer. The process of converting analog signals to digital and back again is called modulation/demodulation. Modem-based transmission is very accurate, despite the fact that telephone lines can be noisy because of clicks, static, and other problems.

Figure 5.25 Modems

An internal modem plugs into an expansion slot on the motherboard. To configure a modem, jumpers may have to be set to select the IRQ and I/O addresses. No configuration is needed for a "plug-and-play" modem, which can only be installed on a motherboard that supports plug and play. A modem using a serial port that is not yet in use must be configured.

Additionally, the software drivers that come with the modem must be installed for the modem to work properly. Drivers for modems are installed the same way drivers are installed for NICs. External modems connect to a computer through the serial and USB ports. When computers use the public telephone system to communicate, this is called dialup networking (DUN). Modems communicate with each other using audio tone signals. This means that modems can duplicate the dialing characteristics of a telephone. DUN creates a Point-to-Point Protocol (PPP) connection between two computers over a phone line. After the line connection has been established, a "handshaking sequence" takes place between the two modems and the computers. The handshaking sequence is a series of short communications that occur between the two systems. This is done to establish the readiness of the two modems and computers to engage in data exchange. Dialup modems send data over the serial telephone line in the form of an analog signal. Because the analog signals change gradually and continuously, they can be drawn as waves. In this system, the digital signals are represented by 1s and 0s. The digital signals must be converted to a waveform to travel across telephone lines. The receiving modem converts them back to digital form, 1s and 0s, so that the receiving computer can process the data.

AT Commands

All modems require software to control the communication session. Most modem software uses the Hayes-compatible command set. The Hayes command set is based on a group of instructions that always begins with a set of attention (AT) characters, followed by the command characters. These are known as AT commands.

The AT commands are modem control commands. The AT command set is used to issue dial, hang-up, reset, and other instructions to the modem. Most user manuals that come with a modem contain a complete listing of the AT command set. The standard Hayes-compatible code to dial is ATD*xxxxxxx*. An AT string usually has no spaces. If a space is inserted, most modems ignore it. The *x* signifies the number dialed. A local call has seven digits, and a long-distance call has 11 digits. A

W indicates that the odem will wait for an outside line, if necessary, to establish a tone before proceeding. Sometimes, a T is added to signify tone dialing, or a P is added to signify pulse dialing.

5.24 OTHER TECHNOLOGIES USED TO ESTABLISH CONNECTIVITY

There are many ways to connect to the Internet. Phone, cable, satellite, and private telecommunications companies offer Internet connections for businesses and home use.

In the 1990s, the Internet typically was used for data transfer. Transmission speeds were slow compared to the high-speed connections that are available today. Most Internet connections were analog modems that used the plain old telephone system (POTS) to send and receive data. In recent years, many businesses and home users have switched to high-speed Internet connections. The additional bandwidth allows for transmission of voice and video as well as data. You should understand how users connect to the Internet and the advantages and disadvantages of different connection types. After completing this section, you will meet these objectives:

♦   Define broadband
♦   Define power line communication
♦   Describe telephone technologies
♦   Define VOIP

Broadband

Broadband is a technique used to transmit and receive multiple signals using multiple frequencies over one cable. For example, the cable used to bring cable television to your home can carry computer network transmissions at the same time. Because the two transmission types use different frequencies, they do not interfere with each other. Broadband is a signaling method that uses a wide range of frequencies that can be further divided into channels. In networking, the term broadband describes communication methods that transmit two or more signals at the same time. Sending two or more signals simultaneously increases the rate of transmission. Some common broadband network connections include cable, DSL, ISDN, and satellite.

Cable

A *cable modem* connects your computer to the cable company using the same coaxial cable that connects to your cable television. You can plug your computer directly into the cable modem, or you can connect a router, switch, hub, or multipurpose network device so that multiple computers can share the connection to the Internet.

DSL

With DSL, the voice and data signals are carried on different frequencies on the copper telephone wires. A filter is used to prevent DSL signals from interfering with phone signals. Plug the filter into a phone jack, and plug the phone into the filter. The DSL modem does not require a filter. The DSL modem is unaffected by the telephone frequencies. Like a cable modem, a DSL modem can connect directly to your computer, or it can be connected to a networking device to share the Internet connection with multiple computers.

ISDN

ISDN is another example of broadband. ISDN uses multiple channels and can carry different types of services; therefore, it is considered a type of broadband. ISDN can carry voice, video, and data.

Satellite

Broadband satellite is an alternative for customers who cannot get cable or DSL connections. A satellite connection does not require a phone line or cable; it uses a satellite dish for two-way communication. Download speeds typically are up to 500 Kbps; uploads are closer to 56 Kbps. It takes time for the signal from the satellite dish to be relayed to your ISP through the satellite orbiting the Earth. People who live in rural areas often use satellite broadband because they need a faster connection than dialup, and no other broadband connection is available.

Power Line Communication

Power line communication (PLC) is a communication method that uses power distribution wires (the local electric grid) to send and receive data, as shown in Figure 5.26.

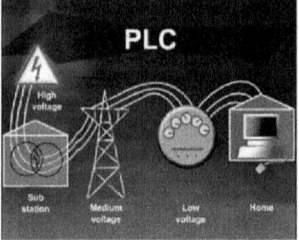

Figure 5.26 Power Line Communication

PLC is known by other names:
♦   Power Line Networking (PLN)
♦   Mains communication
♦   Power Line Telecom (PLT)

With PLC, an electric company can superimpose an analog signal over the standard 50- or 60-Hz AC that travels in power lines. The analog signal can carry voice and data signals. PLC may be available in areas where other high-speed connections are not. PLC is faster than an analog modem and may cost much less than other high-speed connection types. As this technology matures, it will become more common to find and may increase in speed.

You can use PLC to network computers within your home instead of installing network cabling or wireless technology. PLC connections can be used anywhere there is an electrical outlet. You can control lighting and appliances using PLC without installing control wiring.

Telephone Technologies

Several WAN solutions are available for connecting between sites or to the Internet. WAN connection services provide different speeds and levels of service. Before committing to any type of Internet connection, research all the available services to determine the best solution to meet the customer's needs.

Analog Telephone

Analog telephone technology uses standard voice telephone lines. This type of service uses a modem to place a telephone call to another modem at a remote site, such as an *Internet service provider (ISP)*. Using the phone line with an analog modem has two major disadvantages. The first is that the telephone line cannot be used for voice calls while the modem is in use. The second is the limited bandwidth provided by analog phone service. The maximum bandwidth using an analog modem is 56 Kbps, but in reality, it usually is much lower than that. An analog modem is not a good solution for the demands of busy networks. Integrated Services Digital Network (ISDN).

The next advancement in WAN service is ISDN. ISDN is a standard for sending voice, video, and data over normal telephone wires. ISDN technology uses the telephone wires as an analog telephone service. However, ISDN uses digital technology to carry the data. Because it uses digital technology, ISDN provides higher-quality voice and higher-speed data transfer than traditional analog telephone service. ISDN digital connections offer three services: Basic Rate Interface (BRI), Primary Rate Interface (PRI), and Broadband ISDN (BISDN). ISDN uses two different types of communication channels. The B channel is used to carry the informationdata, voice, or video. The D channel usually is used for controlling and signaling, but it can be used for data. Here are the types of ISDN:

♦   **BRI:** ISDN Basic Rate Interface offers a dedicated 128-Kbps connection using two 64-Kbps B channels. ISDN BRI also uses one 16-Kbps D channel for call setup, control, and teardown.

♦   **PRI:** ISDN Primary Rate Interface offers up to 1.544 Mbps over 23 B channels in North America and Japan or 2.048 Mbps over 30 B channels in Europe and Australia. ISDN PRI also uses one 64-Kbps D channel for call maintenance.

♦   **BISDN:** Broadband ISDN manages different types of service all at the same time. BISDN is mostly used only in network backbones.

Digital Subscriber Line (DSL) DSL is an "always-on" technology. This means that you don't need to dial up each time to connect to the Internet. DSL uses the existing copper telephone lines to provide high-speed digital data communication between end users and telephone companies. Unlike ISDN, in which digital data communication replaces analog voice communication, DSL shares the telephone wire with analog signals.

The telephone company limits the bandwidth of the analog voice on the lines. This limit allows the DSL to place digital data on the phone wire in the unused portion of the bandwidth. This sharing of the phone wire allows voice calls to be placed while DSL is connecting to the Internet.

You must consider two major points when selecting DSL. DSL has distance limitations. The phone lines used with DSL were designed to carry analog information. Therefore, the length that the digital signal can be sent is limited, and the signal cannot pass through any form of multiplexer used with analog phone lines. The other consideration is that the voice information and the data carried by DSL must be separated at the customer site. A device called a splitter separates the connection to the phones and the connection to the local network devices. Asymmetric digital subscriber line

(ADSL) is currently the most commonly used DSL technology. ADSL has different bandwidth capabilities in each direction. ADSL has a fast downstream speed typically 1.5 Mbps. Downstream is the process of transferring data from the server to the end user. This is beneficial to users who download large amounts of data. The high-speed upload rate of ADSL is slower. ADSL does not perform well when hosting a web server or FTP server, both of which involve upload-intensive Internet activities.

The following are some of the most common DSL types:

♦   ***ADSL:*** Asymmetric DSL currently is the most common implementation. It has speeds that vary from 384 Kbps to more than 6 Mbps downstream. The upstream speed typically is lower.

♦   ***HDSL:*** High Data Rate DSL provides equal bandwidth in both directions. It is 1.544 Mbps in North America and 2.048 Mbps in Europe.

♦   **SDSL:** Symmetric DSL provides the same speed, up to 3 Mbps, for uploads and downloads.

♦   **VDSL:** Very High Data Rate DSL is capable of bandwidths between 13 and 52 Mbps downstream and 16 Mbps upstream.

♦   ***IDSL:*** ISDN DSL is actually DSL over ISDN lines. It is a set of CCIT/ITU standards for digital transmission over ordinary telephone copper wire, as well as over other media, with a top speed of 144 Kbps. ISDN is available in areas that do not qualify for other DSL implementations. An ISDN adapter at both the user side and service provider side is required. ISDN generally is available in urban areas in the U.S. and Europe from the local phone company.

Define VoIP

Voice over IP (VoIP) is a method to carry telephone calls over the data networks and Internet. VoIP converts the analog signals of our voices into digital information that is transported in IP packets. VoIP can also use an existing IP network to provide access to the public switched telephone network (PSTN). When using VoIP, you are dependent on an Internet connection. This can be a disadvantage if the Internet connection experiences an interruption in service. When a service interruption occurs, the user cannot make phone calls.

Figure 5.27 VoIP Phones

5.25   COMMON PREVENTIVE MAINTENANCE TECHNIQUES USED FOR NETWORKS

Certain common preventive maintenance techniques should continually be performed for a network to operate properly. If an organization has one malfunctioning computer, generally only one user is affected. But if the network is malfunctioning, many or all users will be unable to work.

One of the biggest problems with network devices, especially in the server room, is heat. Network devices, such as computers, hubs, and switches, do not perform well when they overheat. Often, excess heat is generated by accumulated dust and dirty air filters. When dust gathers in and on network devices, it impedes the flow of cool air and sometimes even clogs fans. It is important to keep network rooms clean and to change air filters often. It is also a good idea to have replacement filters available for prompt maintenance.

Preventive maintenance involves checking a network's various components for wear. Check the condition of network cables, because they are often moved, unplugged, and kicked.

Many network problems can be traced to a faulty cable. You should replace any cables that have exposed wires, that are badly twisted, or that are bent.

Label your cables. This practice will save troubleshooting time later. Refer to wiring diagrams, and always follow your company's cable-labeling guidelines.

Troubleshoot a Network
Network issues can be simple or complex. To assess how complicated the problem is, you should determine how many computers on the network are experiencing the problem. If there is a problem with one computer on the network, start the troubleshooting process at that computer. If there is a problem with all computers on the network, start the troubleshooting process in the network room where all computers are connected. As a technician, you should develop a logical and consistent method for diagnosing network problems by eliminating one problem at a time. Follow the steps outlined in this section to accurately identify, repair, and document the problem.

The troubleshooting process is as follows:

Step 1.   Gather data from the customer.

Step 2.   Verify the obvious issues.

Step 3.   Try quick solutions first.

Step 4.   Gather data from the computer.

Step 5.   Evaluate the problem and implement the solution.

Step 6.   Close with the customer.

After completing this section, you will meet these objectives:

♦   Review the troubleshooting process.

♦   Identify common network problems and solutions.

Review the Troubleshooting Process
Network problems can result from a combination of hardware, software, and connectivity issues. Computer technicians must be able to analyze the problem and determine the cause of the error to repair the network issue. This process is called troubleshooting. The first step in the troubleshooting process is to gather data from the customer. Here are some open-ended questions to ask the customer:

♦   What problems are you experiencing with your computer or network?
♦   What software has been installed on your computer recently?
♦   What were you doing when the problem was identified?
♦   What error messages have you received on your computer?
♦   What type of network connection is the computer using?

Here are some closed-ended questions to ask the customer:

♦   Has anyone else used your computer recently?
♦   Can you see any shared files or printers?
♦   Have you changed your password recently?

How To

♦   Can you access the Internet?
♦   Are you currently logged into the network?

After you have talked to the customer, you should verify the obvious issues for networks:

♦   Loose cable connections
♦   Improperly installed NIC
♦   Check the NIC link lights
♦   Low wireless signal strength
♦   Invalid IP address

After you have checked the obvious issues, try some quick solutions for networks:

♦   Check that all cables are connected to the proper locations.
♦   Unseat and then reconnect cables and connectors.
♦   Reboot the computer or network device.
♦   Log in as a different user.
♦   Repair or reenable the network connection.
♦   Contact the network administrator.

If quick solutions do not correct the problem, it is time to gather data from the computer.

Here are some different ways to gather information about the problem from the network:

♦   Ping is used to check network connectivity. It sends a packet to the specified address and waits for a reply.

♦   Nslookup is used to query Internet domain name servers. It returns a list of hosts in a domain or the information for one host.

♦   Tracert is used to determine the route taken by packets when they travel across the network. It shows where communications between your computer and another computer are having difficulty.

♦   Net View displays a list of computers in a workgroup. It shows the available shared resources on a network.

At this point, you have enough information to evaluate the problem and then research and implement possible solutions.

Here are some resources for possible solutions:

♦ Problem-solving experience

Other technicians

♦ Internet search
  Newsgroups
♦ Manufacturer FAQs
♦ Computer manuals
♦ Device manuals
♦ Online forums
♦ Technical websites

After you have solved the network problem, you close with the customer. Here are some of the tasks required to complete this step:

♦ Discuss the solution implemented with the customer.
♦ Have the customer verify that the problem has been solved.
♦ Provide the customer with all the paperwork.
♦ Document the steps taken to solve the problem in the work order and the technician's journal.
♦ Document any components used in the repair.
♦ Document the time spent to resolve the problem.

Identify Common Network Problems and Solutions
Network problems can be attributed to hardware, software, connectivity issues, or some combination of the three. You will resolve some types of network problems more often than others.

Summary
This chapter introduced you to the fundamentals of networking, the benefits of having a network, and the ways to connect computers to a network. The different aspects of troubleshooting a network were discussed, with examples of how to analyze and implement simple solutions. The following concepts from this chapter are important to remember:

♦ A computer network is composed of two or more computers that share data and resources.

♦ A local-area network (LAN) is a group of interconnected computers that are under the same administrative control.

♦ A wide-area network (WAN) connects LANs in geographically separated locations.

♦ In a peer-to-peer network, devices are connected directly to each other. A peer-to-peer network is easy to install, and no additional equipment or dedicated administrator is required.

♦ The network topology defines how computers, printers, and other devices are connected. The physical topology describes the layout of the wire and devices, as well as the paths used by data transmissions. The logical topology is the path that signals travel from one point to another. Topologies include bus, star, ring, and mesh.

♦ Networking media can be defined as the means by which signals, or data, are sent from one computer to another. Signals can be transmitted by either cable or wireless means. The media types discussed were coaxial cable, twisted-pair cable, fiber-optic cable, and radio frequencies.

♦ Ethernet architecture is currently the most popular type of LAN architecture.

♦ The OSI reference model is an industry-standard framework that is used to divide networking functions into seven distinct layers: application, presentation, session, transport, network, data link, and physical. It is important to understand the purpose of each layer.

♦ The TCP/IP suite of protocols has become the dominant standard for the Internet.

♦ A NIC is a device that plugs into a motherboard and provides ports for the network cable connections. It is the computer interface with the LAN.

♦ The three transmission methods for sending signals over data channels are simplex, half duplex, and full duplex. Full-duplex networking technology increases performance because data can be sent and received at the same time. DSL, two-way cable modem, and other broadband technologies operate in full-duplex mode.

♦ It is important to clean equipment regularly and to use a proactive approach to prevent problems.

♦ When troubleshooting network problems, listen to what your customer tells you so that you can formulate open-ended and closed-ended questions that will help you determine where to begin fixing the problem. Verify obvious issues, and try quick solutions before escalating the troubleshooting process.

REVISION QUESTIONS

1. Which cable type is a common choice for use on Ethernet networks?
   A. Thick coaxial
   B. UTP
   C. STP
   D. Thin coaxial

2. Which dotted-decimal number is used to distinguish the network portion of the IP address from the host portion?
   A. Subnet mask
   B. Default gateway
   C. Physical address
   D. MAC address

3. Which suite of protocols is used to transmit data across the Internet?
   A. AppleTalk
   B. TCP/IP
   C. DNS

    D.   IPX/SPX

    E.   ARP

4.   The Internet is an example of which type of network?

    A.   LAN

    B.   WAN

    C.   SAN

    D.   WLAN

5.   What is the suggested maximum number of PCs in a peer-to-peer network?

    A.   50

    B.   25

    C.   100

    D.   10

6.   A technician wants to update the NIC driver for a computer. What is the best way to find new drivers for the NIC?

    A.   Installation media that came with the NIC

    B.   The website for the manufacturer of the NIC

    C.   Windows Update

    D.   The Microsoft website

CHAPTER SIX

NETWORK SECURITY

6.1   INTRODUCTION

Technicians need to understand computer and network security. Failure to implement proper security procedures can affect users, computers, and the general public. Private information, company secrets, financial data, computer equipment, and items of national security are placed at risk if proper security procedures are not followed.

6.2   WHY SECURITY IS IMPORTANT

Computer and network security help keep data and equipment safe by giving only the appropriate people access. Everyone in an organization should give high priority to security, because everyone can be affected by a lapse in security. Theft, loss, network intrusion, and physical damage are some of the ways a network or computer can be harmed. Damage or loss of equipment can mean a loss of productivity. Repairing and replacing equipment can cost the company time and money. Unauthorized duse of a network can expose confidential information and reduce network resources.

An attack that intentionally degrades the performance of a computer or network can also harm an organization's production. Poorly implemented security measures that allow unauthorized access to wireless network devices demonstrate that physical connectivity is not necessary for security breaches by intruders.

A technician's primary responsibilities include data and network security. A customer or an organization may depend on you to ensure that their data and computer equipment are secure. You will perform tasks that are more sensitive than those assigned to the average employee. You may have to repair, adjust, and install equipment. You need to know how to configure settings to keep the network secure, but still keep it available to those who need to access it. You will ensure that software patches and updates are applied, antivirus software is installed, and antispyware software is used. You may also be asked to instruct users on how to maintain good security practices with computer equipment.

In this activity, you use the Internet, a newspaper, or magazines to gather information to help you become familiar with computer crime and security attacks in your area. Be prepared to discuss your research with the class

6.3   NETWORK SECURITY THREATS

To successfully protect computers and the network, a technician must understand both of the following types of threats to computer security:

♦   **Physical:** Events or attacks that steal, damage, or destroy such equipment as servers, switches, and wiring.

♦   **Data:** Events or attacks that remove, corrupt, deny access to, allow access to, or steal information. Threats to security can come from inside or outside an organization, and the level of potential damage can vary greatly. Potential threats include the following:

♦   **Internal:** Employees who have access to data, equipment, and the network. Internal attacks can be characterized as follows:

♦   *Malicious Threats* are when an employee intends to cause damage.

♦   *Accidental Threats* are when the user damages data or equipment unintentionally.

♦   **External:** Users outside an organization who do not have authorized access to the network or resources. External attacks can be characterized as follows:

♦   Unstructured attacks, which use available resources, such as passwords or scripts, to gain access to and run programs designed to vandalize.

♦   Structured attacks, which use code to access operating systems and software. Physical loss or damage to equipment can be expensive, and data loss can be detrimental to your business and reputation. Threats against data are constantly changing as attackers find new ways to gain entry and commit their crimes. After completing this section, you will meet these objectives:

♦   Define viruses, worms, and Trojan horses.
♦   Explain web security.
♦   Define adware, spyware, and grayware.
♦   Explain denial of service.
♦   Describe spam and popups.
♦   Explain social engineering.
♦   Explain TCP/IP attacks.
♦   Explain hardware deconstruction and recycling.

6.4   THE VIRUSES, WORMS, AND TROJAN HORSES

Computer viruses are created with malicious intent and sent by attackers. A *virus* is attached to small pieces of computer code, software, or documents. The virus executes when the software is run on a computer. If the virus spreads to other computers, those computers could continue to spread the virus.

A virus is transferred to another computer through e-mail, file transfers, and instant messaging. The virus hides by attaching itself to a file on the computer. When the file is accessed, the virus executes and infects the computer. A virus has the potential to corrupt or even delete files on your computer, use your e-mail to spread itself to other computers, or even erase your hard drive.

Some viruses can be exceptionally dangerous. The most damaging type of virus is used to record keystrokes. Attackers can use these viruses to harvest sensitive information, such as passwords and credit card numbers. Viruses may even alter or destroy information on a computer. Stealth viruses can infect a computer and lay dormant until summoned by the attacker.

A *worm* is a self-replicating program that is harmful to networks. A worm uses the network to duplicate its code to the hosts on a network, often without any user intervention. It is different from a virus because a worm does not need to attach to a program to infect a host. Even if the worm does not damage data or applications on the hosts it infects, it harms networks because it consumes bandwidth.

A *Trojan horse* technically is a worm. It does not need to be attached to other software. Instead, a Trojan threat is hidden in software that appears to do one thing, and yet behind the scenes it does another. Trojans often are disguised as useful software. The Trojan program can reproduce like a virus and spread to other computers. Computer data damage and production loss could be significant. A technician may be needed to perform the repairs, and employees may lose or have to replace data. An infected computer could be sending critical data to competitors while at the same time infecting other computers on the network.

Virus protection software, known as *antivirus software*, is software designed to detect, disable, and remove viruses, worms, and Trojans before they infect a computer. Antivirus software becomes outdated quickly, however. The technician is responsible for applying the most recent updates, patches, and virus definitions as part of a regular maintenance schedule.

Many organizations establish a written *security policy* stating that employees are not permitted to install any software that is not provided by the company. Organizations also make employees aware of the dangers of opening e-mail attachments that may contain a virus or worm.

In this activity, you use the Internet, a newspaper, or a local store to gather information about third-party antivirus software.

6.5   WEB SECURITY

Web security is important because so many people visit the World Wide Web every day. Some of the features that make the web useful and entertaining can also make it harmful to a computer.

Tools that are used to make web pages more powerful and versatile can also make computers more vulnerable to attacks. Here are some examples of web tools:

♦   *ActiveX* is technology created by Microsoft to control interactivity on web pages. If ActiveX is on a page, the user must download an applet or small program to gain access to the full functionality.

♦   *Java* is a programming language that allows applets to run within a web browser. Examples of applets include a calculator and a counter.

♦   *JavaScript* is a programming language developed to interact with HTML source code to allow interactive websites. Examples include a rotating banner and a popup window. Attackers can use any of these tools to install a program on a computer. To protect against these attacks, most browsers have settings that force the computer user to authorize the downloading or use of ActiveX, Java, and JavaScript.

Define Adware, Spyware, and Grayware

Adware, spyware, and grayware are usually installed on a computer without the user's knowledge. These programs collect information stored on the computer, change the computer configuration, or open extra windows on the computer without the user's consent.

Adware is a software program that displays advertising on your computer. Adware is usually distributed with downloaded software. Most often, adware is displayed in a popup window. Adware popup windows are sometimes difficult to control; they open new windows faster than users can close them.

Grayware or *malware* is a file or program other than a virus that is potentially harmful. Many grayware attacks are phishing attacks, which try to persuade the user to unknowingly give attackers access to personal information. As you fill out an online form, the data is sent to the attacker. Grayware can be removed using spyware and adware removal tools.

Spyware, a type of grayware, is similar to adware. It is distributed without any user intervention or knowledge. After it is installed, the spyware monitors activity on the computer. The spyware then sends this information to the organization responsible for launching the spyware.

Phishing is a form of *social engineering*, in which the attacker pretends to represent a legitimate outside organization, such as a bank. A potential victim is contacted via e-mail. The attacker might ask for verification of information, such as a password or username, to supposedly prevent some terrible consequence from occurring.

Note: There is rarely a need to give out sensitive personal or financial information online. Be suspicious. Use the postal service to share sensitive information.

Denial of Service

Denial of service (DoS) is a form of attack that prevents users from accessing normal services, such as e-mail or a web server. DoS works by sending so many requests for a system resource that the requested service is overloaded and ceases to operate. DoS attacks can affect servers and computers in the following ways:

♦   *Ping of death* is a series of repeated, larger-than-normal pings that are intended to crash the receiving computer.

♦   An *e-mail bomb* is a large quantity of bulk e-mail sent to individuals, lists, or domains, intending to prevent users from accessing e-mail.

Distributed DoS (DDoS) is another form of attack that uses many infected computers, called zombies, to launch an attack. With DDoS, the intent is to obstruct or overwhelm access to the targeted server. Zombie computers located at different geographic locations make it difficult to trace the origin of the attack.

Spam and Popup Windows

Spam, also known as junk mail, is unsolicited e-mail. In most cases, spam is used for advertising.

However, spam can be used to send harmful links or deceptive content. When used as an attack method, spam might include links to an infected website or an attachment that could infect a computer. These links or attachments might generate lots of windows (called *popups*) designed to capture your attention and lead you to advertising sites. Uncontrolled popup windows can quickly cover your screen and prevent you from getting any work done.

Many antivirus and e-mail software programs automatically detect and remove spam from an e-mail inbox. Some spam still may get through, so you should look for some of the more common indications:

♦   No subject line

♦   An incomplete return addresses

♦   Computer-generated e-mails

♦   Return e-mails not sent by the user

6.6   SOCIAL ENGINEERING

A social engineer is a person who gains access to equipment or a network by tricking people into providing the necessary information. Often, the social engineer gains the confidence of an employee and convinces that person to divulge username and password information. A social engineer may pose as a technician to try to gain entry into a facility. When he is inside, he may look over employees' shoulders to gather information, seek out papers on desks with passwords and phone extensions, or obtain a company directory with e-mail addresses.

The following are some basic precautions to help protect against social engineering:

♦   Never give out your password.

♦   Always ask for the ID of unknown persons.

♦   Restrict the access of unexpected visitors.

♦   Escort all visitors.

♦   Never post your password in your work area.

♦   Log off or lock your computer when you leave your desk.

♦   Do not let anyone follow you through a door that requires an access card.

TCP/IP Attacks

TCP/IP is the protocol suite that is used to control all the communications on the Internet. Unfortunately, TCP/IP can also make a network available to attackers through the use of the following common types of attacks:

♦   A *SYN flood* randomly opens TCP ports, tying up network equipment or a computer with a large number of false requests, causing sessions to be denied to others.

♦   **DoS** attempts to make a computer resource unavailable to its intended users.

♦   **DDoS** is a DoS attack that uses "zombies" to make tracing the origin of the attack difficult.

♦   *Spoofing* is a method of gaining access to resources on devices by pretending to be a trusted computer.

♦   **Man-in-the-middle** intercepts or inserts false information in traffic between two hosts.

♦   *Replay* uses network sniffers to extract usernames and passwords to be used later to gain access.

♦   ***DNS poisoning*** changes the DNS records on a system to point to false servers where the data
is recorded.

Hardware Deconstruction and Recycling
Hardware deconstruction is the process of removing sensitive data from hardware and software
before recycling or discarding them. Hard drives should be erased to prevent someone from
recovering the data using specialized software. It is not enough to delete files or even format the
drive. Use a third-party tool to overwrite data multiple times, rendering the data unusable. The only
way to be certain that data cannot be recovered from a hard drive is to carefully shatter the platters
with a hammer and safely dispose of the pieces. Media such as CDs and floppy disks must also be
destroyed. Use a shredding machine that is designed for this purpose.

Security Procedures
You should use a security plan to determine what will be done in a critical situation. Security plan
policies should be constantly updated to reflect the latest threats to a network. A security plan with
clear security procedures is the basis for a technician to follow. Security plans should be reviewed
each year.

Part of the process of ensuring security is conducting tests to determine areas where security is
weak. Testing should be done on a regular basis. New threats are released daily. Regular testing
provides details of any possible weaknesses in the current security plan that should be addressed.

A network has multiple layers of security, as shown in Figure 6.1, including physical, wireless, and
data. Each layer is subject to security attacks. The technician needs to understand how to implement
security procedures to protect equipment and data.

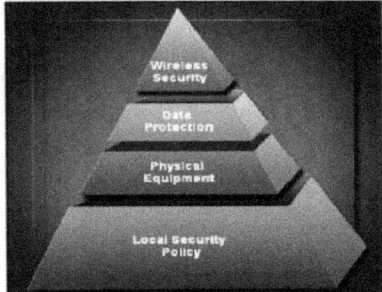

Figure 6.1 Security Pyramid

After completing this section, you will meet these objectives:
♦   Explain what is required in a basic local security policy.
♦   Explain the tasks required to protect physical equipment.
♦   Describe ways to protect data.
♦   Describe wireless security techniques.

What Is Required in a Basic Local Security Policy

Although local security policies may vary between organizations, all organizations should ask the following questions:

♦   What assets require protection?

♦   What are the possible threats?

♦   What should be done in the event of a security breach?

A security policy should describe how a company defines security issues:

♦   A process for handling network security incidents

♦   A process for auditing existing network security

♦   A general security framework for implementing network security

♦   Behaviors that are allowed

♦   Behaviors that are prohibited

♦   What to log and how to store the logs: Event Viewer, system log files, or security log files

♦   Network access to resources through account permissions

♦   Authentication technologies (such as usernames, passwords, biometrics, and smart cards) to access data

6.7   THE TASKS REQUIRED PROTECTING PHYSICAL EQUIPMENT

Physical security is as important as data security. When a computer is stolen, the data is also stolen. There are several ways to physically protect computer equipment:

♦   Control access to facilities.

♦   Use cable locks with equipment, as shown in Figure 6.2.

♦   Keep telecommunication rooms locked.

♦   Fit equipment with security screws, as shown in Figure 6.2.

♦   Use security cages around equipment, as shown in Figure 6.3.

♦   Label and install sensors, such as Radio Frequency Identification (RFID) tags, on equipment.

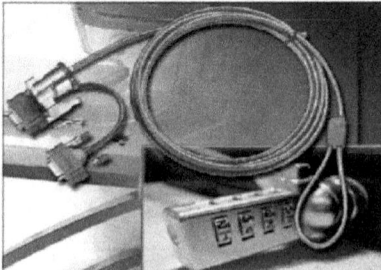

Figure 6.2 Physical Security

Figure 6.3 Locking Devices

For access to facilities, there are several means of protection:

♦   *Card keys* that store user data, including level of access

♦   *Biometric* sensors that identify the user's physical characteristics, such as fingerprints or retinas

♦   Posted security guard

♦   Sensors, such as RFID tags, to monitor equipment

Ways to Protect Data

The value of physical equipment is often far less than the value of the data it contains. The loss of sensitive data to a company's competitors or to criminals may be costly. Such losses may result in a lack of confidence in the company and the dismissal of computer technicians in charge of computer security. To protect data, you can implement several methods of security protection, as described in the following sections.

Password Protection
Password protection can prevent unauthorized access to content, as shown in Figure 6.4.

♦   To keep attackers from gaining access to data, all computers should be password-protected. Two levels of password protection are recommended:

♦   **BIOS** prevents BIOS settings from being changed without the appropriate password.

♦   **Login** prevents unauthorized access to the network.

Figure 6.4 Secured Connection

Network logins provide a means of logging activity on the network and either preventing or allowing access to resources. This makes it possible to determine what resources are being accessed. Usually, the system administrator defines a naming convention for the usernames when creating network logins. A common example of a username is the person's first initial and last name. You should keep the username naming convention simple so that people do not have a hard time remembering it.

When passwords are assigned, the level of password control should match the level of protection required. A good security policy should be strictly enforced and should include, but not be limited to, the following rules:

♦ Passwords should expire after a specific period of time.

♦ Passwords should contain a mixture of numbers, special characters, and uppercase and lowercase letters so that they cannot easily be broken. They should have a minimum of eight characters.

♦ Users should not write down passwords and leave them where anyone can find them.

♦ Rules about password expiration and lockout should be defined. Lockout rules apply when an unsuccessful attempt has been made to access the system or when a specific change has been detected in the system configuration.

To simplify the process of administering security, it is common to assign users to groups and then assign groups to resources. This allows you to easily change the access level of users on a network by assigning the users to or removing them from various groups. This is useful when setting up temporary accounts for visiting workers or consultants, giving you the ability to limit access to resources.

Data Encryption
Encrypting data involves using codes and ciphers. ***Data encryption*** can help prevent attackers from monitoring or recording traffic between resources and computers. It may not be possible to decipher captured data in time to make any use of it. A security alert may inform you that you are using an encrypted connection.

A virtual private network (VPN) is an encryption system that protects data as though it resides on a private network. The data actually travels over the Internet or another unsecured public network.

Port Protection
Every communication using TCP/IP is associated with a port number. HTTPS, for instance, by default uses port 443. A firewall, as illustrated in Figure 6-5, is a way of protecting a computer from intrusion through the ports.

Figure 6.5 Firewall

With ***port protection***, the user can control the type of data sent to a computer by selecting which ports will be open and which will be secured. Data being transported on a network is called *traffic*. Table 9-1 shows the ports and protocols associated with the more common types of traffic.

Data Backups

You should include data backup procedures in a security plan. Data can be lost or damaged in circumstances such as theft or equipment failure, or in a disaster, such as a fire or flood.

Backing up data is one of the most effective ways of protecting against data loss. Here are some considerations for ***data backups***:

♦   **Frequency of backups:** Backups can take a long time. Sometimes it is easier to make a full backup monthly or weekly and then do frequent partial backups of any data that has changed since the last full backup. However, spreading the backups over many recordings increases the amount of time needed to restore the data.

♦   **Storing backups:** Backups should be transported to an approved offsite storage location for extra security. The current backup medium is transported to the offsite location on a daily, weekly, or monthly rotation, as required by the local organization.

♦   **Security of backups:** Backups can be protected with passwords. These passwords have to be entered before the data on the backup media can be restored.

File System Security

All file systems keep track of resources, but only file systems with journals can log access by user, date, and time. FAT32, which is used in some versions of the Windows file system, lacks both journaling and encryption capabilities. As a result, situations that require good security are usually deployed using a file system such as NTFS, which is part of Windows 2000 and Windows XP. When increased ***file system security*** is needed, it is possible to run certain utilities, such as CONVERT, to upgrade a FAT32 file system to NTFS. The conversion process is not reversible. It is important to define your goals clearly before making the transition.

6.8   WIRELESS SECURITY TECHNIQUES

Traffic flows through radio waves in wireless networks, so it is easy for attackers to monitor and attack data without having to connect to a network physically. Attackers gain access to a network by being within range of an unprotected wireless network. A technician needs to know how to configure access points and wireless network interface cards (WNIC) to an appropriate level of security. When installing wireless services, you should apply the following wireless security techniques immediately to prevent unwanted access to the network:

♦   ***Wired Equivalent Privacy (WEP)*** was the first-generation security standard for wireless. Attackers quickly discovered that 64-bit WEP encryption was easy to break. Monitoring programs could detect the encryption keys used to encode the messages. After the keys were obtained, messages could be easily decoded. In an attempt to overcome this weakness, most users employ a 128-bit key for WEP.

♦ Change the default administration password.

♦ Disable the broadcasting of the Service Set Identifier (SSID) to hide it from other users.

♦ Use MAC filtering to protect the network from other users.

♦ Change the default values of the SSID by entering the setup program for the access point and renaming the SSID.

♦ Update to the latest available firmware.

♦ Install or activate a firewall, and adjust the settings to eliminate all traffic except the desired network settings.

♦ Update to the latest available firmware.

♦ Install or activate a firewall, and adjust the settings to eliminate all traffic except the desired network settings.

An attacker can access data as it travels over the radio signal. However, you can use a wireless encryption system to encode data and thereby prevent unwanted capture and use of the data. Both ends of every link must use the same encryption standard. The following list describes the different levels of wireless security, from most secure to least secure:

♦ **_Lightweight Extensible Authentication Protocol (LEAP)_**: Also called EAP-Cisco, LEAP is a wireless security protocol created by Cisco to address the weaknesses in WEP and WPA. LEAP is a good choice when using Cisco equipment in conjunction with operating systems such as Windows and Linux.

♦ **_Wi-Fi Protected Access (WPA)_**: An improved version of WEP. It was created as a temporary solution until 802.11i (a security layer for wireless systems) was fully implemented. Now that 802.11i has been ratified, WPA2 has been released. It covers the entire 802.11i standard.

♦ **WEP 128:** An enhanced encryption protocol combining a 104-bit key and a 24-bit initialization vector.

♦ **WEP 64:** The first-generation security standard for wireless. It could be exploited because of an encryption key that was vulnerable to decoding.

♦ **No security:** Although you can elect to implement no security whatsoever, you leave your wireless network completely vulnerable to attack.

In addition, **_Wireless Transport Layer Security (WTLS)_** is a security layer used in mobile devices that employ the Wireless Applications Protocol (WAP). Mobile devices do not have a great deal of spare bandwidth to devote to security protocols. WTLS was designed to provide security for WAP devices in a bandwidth-efficient manner.

6.9   COMMON PREVENTIVE MAINTENANCE TECHNIQUES FOR SECURITY

Regular security updates are essential to meet the threat from attackers constantly searching for new ways of breaching security. Software manufacturers have to regularly create and issue new patches to fix flaws and vulnerabilities in products. If a technician leaves a computer unprotected, an attacker can easily gain access. Unprotected computers on the Internet may become infected within a few minutes.

Because of the constantly changing security threats, a technician should understand how to install patches and updates, as shown in Figure 6.6. They should also be able to recognize when new updates and patches are available. Some manufacturers release updates on the same day every month and also send out critical updates when necessary. Other manufacturers provide automatic update services that patch the software every time a computer is turned on. Manufacturers also often send e-mail notifications when a new patch or update is released.

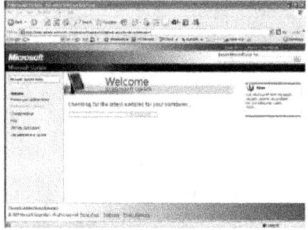

Figure 6.6 Security Updates

At the end of this section, you will meet these objectives:

♦   Explain how to update signature files for virus checkers and spyware.

♦   Explain how to install operating system service packs and security patches.

How to Update Signature Files for Virus Checkers and Spyware

Threats to security from viruses and worms are always present. Attackers constantly look for new ways to infiltrate computers and networks. Because new viruses are always being developed, security software must be continually updated. This process can be performed automatically, but a technician should know how to manually update any type of protection software and all customer application programs. Virus, spyware, and adware detection programs look for patterns in the programming code of the software in a computer. These patterns are determined by analyzing viruses that are intercepted on the Internet and on local-area networks (LAN). These code patterns are called signatures. The publishers of protection software compile the signatures into virus definition tables. To update *signature files* for antivirus and antispyware software, first check to see if the signature files are the most recent ones. You can do this by navigating to the **About** option of the protection software or by launching the update tool for the protection software. If the signature files are out of date, update them manually with the **Update Now** option available on most protection software.

You should always retrieve the signature files from the manufacturer's website. However, to avoid creating too much traffic at a single site, some manufacturers distribute the signature files for download to multiple download sites. These download sites are called mirrors.

To update a signature file, follow these steps:

Step 1:   Set the Windows restore point.

Step 2:   Open the antivirus or antispyware program.

Step 3:   Locate the update control button, and select it.

Step 4: After the program is updated, use it to scan your computer.
Step 5:   When the scan is complete, check the report for viruses or other problems that could not be treated, and delete them yourself.
Step 6: Set the antivirus or antispyware program to automatically update and to run on a scheduled basis.

Caution

When downloading the signature files from a mirror, ensure that the mirror site is legitimate. Always link to the mirror site from the manufacturer's website.

How To
How to Install Operating System Service
Packs and Security Patches

Viruses and worms can be difficult to remove from a computer. Software tools are required to remove viruses and repair the computer code that the virus has modified. These software tools are provided by operating system manufacturers and security software companies.

Make sure that you download these tools from a legitimate site.

Manufacturers of operating systems and software applications may provide code updates called patches that prevent a newly discovered virus or worm from making a successful attack. From time to time, manufacturers combine patches and upgrades into a comprehensive update application called a service pack. Many infamous and devastating virus attacks could have been much less severe if more users had downloaded and installed the latest service pack.

The Windows operating system routinely checks the Windows Update website for high-priority updates that can help protect a computer from the latest security threat. These updates can include security updates, critical updates, and service packs. Depending on the setting you choose, Windows automatically downloads and installs any high-priority updates that your computer needs, or notifies you as these updates become available. Updates must be installed, not just downloaded. If you use the Automatic setting, you can schedule the time and day. Otherwise, new updates are installed at 3 a.m. by default. If your computer is turned off during a scheduled update, updates are installed the next time you start your computer. You can also choose to have Windows notify you when a new update is available and install the update yourself. To update the operating system with a service pack or security patch, follow these steps:

Step 1:   Create a restore point in case of a problem with the update.
Step 2:   Check the updates to ensure that you have the latest ones.
Step 3:   Download the updates using Automatic Updates or from the operating system manufacturer's website.
Step 4:   Install the update.
Step 5:   Restart if required.
Step 6:   Test all aspects to ensure that the update has not caused any issues.

How To
Troubleshoot Security

The troubleshooting process is used to help resolve security issues. These problems range from simple, such as preventing someone from watching over your shoulder, to more complex problems, such as manually removing infected files. Use the troubleshooting steps as a guideline to help diagnose and repair problems. After completing this section, you will meet these objectives:

♦ Review the troubleshooting process.
♦ Identify common problems and solutions.

Review the Troubleshooting Process
Computer technicians must be able to analyze a security threat and determine the appropriate method to protect assets and repair damage. This process is called *troubleshooting*.

Step 1: Gather Data from the Customer
  The first step in the troubleshooting process is to gather   data from the customer.

Step 2: Verify the Obvious Issues
  After you have talked to the customer, you should verify the obvious issues. Here are some issues that apply to   laptops:

♦ Have people asked you to stop sending them strange e-mails even though you have not sent them anything?
♦ Have any items on your desktop been moved?
♦ Has your computer been running slower than normal, or is it unresponsive?
♦ Do you see any unfamiliar login addresses in the login window?
♦ Are there any unexplained entries in the security protection software logs?
♦ Is your Internet connection unusually slow?

Step 3: Try Quick Solutions First
  After you have verified the obvious issues, try some   quick solutions:

♦ Reboot the computer or network device.
♦ Log in as a different user.
♦ Check that the antivirus and spyware signature files are up-to-date.
♦ Scan the computer with protection software.
♦ Check the computer for the latest operating system patches and updates.
♦ Disconnect from the network.
♦ Change your password.

Step 4: Gather Data from the Computer
  If quick solutions do not correct the problem, it is time to gather data from the computer:
♦ Verify that the signature file is current.
♦ Check the security software log file for entries.
Step 5: Evaluate the Problem and Implement the Solution

At this point, you have enough information to evaluate the problem and to research and implement possible solutions. Here are some resources for possible solutions:

♦ Problem-solving experience

Other technicians

♦   Internet search

♦   Newsgroups

♦   Manufacturer FAQs

♦   Computer manuals

♦   Device manuals

Online forums

♦   Technical websites

Step 6: Close with the Customer

After you have solved the problem, you close with the   customer. Here   are   the   steps required to complete this   task:

Step 1.   Discuss the solution implemented with the customer.

Step 2.   Have the customer verify that the problem has been solved.

Step 3.   Provide the customer with all the paperwork.

Step 4.   Document the steps taken to solve the problem in the work order and the technician's journal.

Step 5.   Document any components used in the repair.

Step 6.   Document the time spent to resolve the problem.

Identify Common Problems and Solutions

Maintaining a computer can be a challenge. One of the biggest challenges is making sure that your computer software is updated and secure.

Possible Security Issue Possible Solution

A computer runs updates and Set Windows Automatic Update to run daily at a requires rebooting at inconvenient convenient time, such as lunchtime. times. A wireless network is compromised Upgrade to 128-bit WEP security, WAP, or even though 64-bit WEP encryption EAP-Cisco security.

How To

The police return a stolen laptop. After recovering any sensitive data, destroy the hard drive. The user no longer needs it. drive and recycle the computer.

A user complains that his system this may be a denial-of-service attack. At the e-mail receives hundreds or thousands of server, filter out e-mail from the sender. junk e-mails daily.

A printer repair person no one Contact security or the police. Advice users never to remembers seeing before is hide passwords near their work area. observed looking under keyboards and on desktops.

Remote Technician 6.5.2: Gather Information from the Customer

In this Remote Technician Activity, you gather data from the customer to begin the troubleshooting process and document the customer's problem in the work order provided in the activity.

Possible Security Issue Possible Solution
Summary
This chapter discussed computer security and why it is important to protect computer equipment, networks, and data. Threats, procedures, and preventive maintenance relating to data and physical security were described to help you keep computer equipment and data safe. Security protects computers, network equipment, and data from loss and physical danger.

The following are some of the important concepts to remember from this chapter:

♦   Security threats can come from inside or outside an organization.

♦   Viruses and worms are common threats that attack data.

♦   Develop and maintain a security plan to protect both data and physical equipment from loss.

♦   Keep operating systems and applications up to date and secure with patches and service packs.

REVISION QUESTIONS

1.   Which step should a technician perform first when troubleshooting security issues?
     A.   Evaluate the problem.
     B.   Gather data from the customer.
     C.   Gather data from the computer.
     D.   Verify the obvious issues.

2.   Which of the following is an encryption system that protects data as if it is on a private network, even though the data is actually traveling over the Internet or other unsecured public networks?
     A.   Data encryption   B.   File system security
     C.   Virtual private network   D.   Port protection

3.   Which type of security threat uses e-mail that appears to be from a legitimate sender and asks the e-mail recipient to visit a website to enter confidential information?
     A.   Stealth virus   B.   Phishing   C.   Badware   D.   Worm

4.   Which type of security threat installs to a computer without the user's knowledge and then monitors all computer activity?
     A.   Grayware   B.   Adware   C.   Malware   D.   Spyware

5.   Which of the following is technically a worm and is a threat that is hidden in software that appears to do one thing, but does another?
     A.   Adware   B.   Spyware   C.   Trojan   D.   Virus

6.   Which of the following is a software program that displays advertising on your computer?
     A.   Virus   B.   Spyware   C.   Adware   D.   Grayware

REFERENCES

Troubleshooting & Maintaining your PC All-in-One for Dummies 2nd Edition, Dan Gooking. Publisher: for Dummies; 2nd Edition (2011).

Hardware Upgrading and Repairing PCs, 19th Edition, Scott Mueller. Publisher: Que; 19th Edition (2009)

Computer Architecture, 5th Edition. Publisher: Morgan Kaufmann; 5th Edition (2011)

Absolute Beginner's Guide to Computer Basics, 5th Edition, Michael Miller Publisher: Que; 5th Edition (2009)

CompTIA ©A+220-801 and 220-802 Authorized Exam cram, 6th Edition, Publisher: Pearson IT Certification; 6th Edition (2012)

Basic Computer Free University of Bolzano Bozen, Dr. Paolo Coletti Edition 7.0 (2012)

Computer Hardware Text Book: Intermediate Vocational Course-1st Year, Smt. D. Fatima M.C.A (M. Tech C. S) (2005)

Computer Theory and Practice, Analyst Odion J. O. Okundia Publisher Justice Jeco Press and Publishers Ltd. (2005).

PC Hardware: A Beginner's Guide Osborne/Mc Graw-Hill (2001)

World Computer Science/Brigham Narins, edition. Publisher: Gale Group/Thomson Learning, (2002).

IT Essentials: PC Hardware and Software Companion Guide: Third Edition, Published by: Cisco Press David Anfinson & Ken Quamme (2008).

INDEX